German Unification
and EC Integration

CHATHAM HOUSE PAPERS

A European Programme Publication
Programme Director: Susie Symes

The Royal Institute of International Affairs, at Chatham House in London, has provided an impartial forum for discussion and debate on current international issues for some 70 years. Its resident research fellows, specialized information resources, and range of publications, conferences, and meetings span the fields of international politics, economics, and security. The Institute is independent of government.

Chatham House Papers are short monographs on current policy problems which have been commissioned by the RIIA. In preparing the papers, authors are advised by a study group of experts convened by the RIIA, and publication of a paper indicates that the Institute regards it as an authoritative contribution to the public debate. The Institute does not, however, hold opinions of its own; the views expressed in this publication are the responsibility of the authors.

CHATHAM HOUSE PAPERS

German Unification and EC Integration
German and British Perspectives

**Barbara Lippert,
Rosalind Stevens-Ströhmann
Dirk Günther, Grit Viertel
and Stephen Woolcock**

The Royal Institute of International Affairs

Pinter Publishers
London

Pinter Publishers Limited
25 Floral Street, Covent Garden, London WC2E 9DS, United Kingdom

First published in 1993

© Royal Institute of International Affairs, 1993

British Library Cataloguing in Publication Data
A CIP catalogue record for this book is available from the British Library

ISBN 1-85567-074-7 (Paperback)
     1-85567-073-9 (Hardback)

Typeset by Koinonia Limited
Printed and bound in Great Britain by
Biddles Limited, Guildford and King's Lynn

CONTENTS

FOREWORD

The idea for this volume was conceived in the period of heady optimism that followed the breaching of the Berlin Wall. Staff at the Institut für Europäische Politik in Bonn and the Royal Institute of International Affairs in London decided that a joint study of German unification, monitoring a historic process, would be a challenging exercise in British–German collaboration. The generous funding from the Anglo-German Foundation for the Study of Industrial Society enabled the project team to experience at close quarters both the positive achievements and some of the frustrations of those engaged in rebuilding a unified Germany.

We deliberately adopted a down-to-earth approach, choosing to examine many of the practical tasks to be confronted within Germany and by the European Community, especially by working on several case-studies. Our reasoning was that this would give us insights into and evidence about how far Germany was being changed by the process, whether this would trigger fundamental reappraisals of European integration and what the impact would be on the German–British relationship. Our approach enabled us to delve below the surface of the sometimes unreal rhetoric of the debate in 1990. It also encouraged a measured prudence on our part, as the costs of unification rose and as the projected timescale for the transformation of the eastern Länder lengthened.

We also had a compelling interest in relations between Britain and Germany and the differences of attitudes in the two countries towards European integration. West Germans were at pains to point out the continuity of German attachment to the European Community and its 'deepening'. Many British were less than convinced, somehow expecting that Germany would be so fundamentally altered by unification that the EC would never be the same again. Some thought that Germany would be weakened and distracted; others that it would be dangerously strengthened to the detriment of British interests.

The completion of the volume in the difficult days of late autumn 1992 makes it particularly hard to draw clear-headed conclusions. The German economy is bearing a heavy burden of adjustment, which spills over into the wider European economy. Political adjustment in both parts of Germany has thrown up some disturbing tensions. Many Germans have come to question the wisdom of European economic and monetary union. Yet Germany has remained on balance a very predictable and accommodating partner in Brussels. Meanwhile Britain has emerged as in many ways the more troubled partner, as the currency crisis of autumn 1992 erupted and as the debate on the ratification of the Maastricht Treaty dragged on. The Bonn–London relationship has indeed been subjected to severe strains.

As for the EC, the immediate and practical contribution of Community institutions, and of some dedicated individuals working within them, to solving problems raised by German unification has been impressive. The fact that the Intergovernmental Conferences which led to Maastricht were kick-started by fears about German unification has almost been forgotten during the febrile debates of 1992. It is disturbing that a gulf persists between German and British attitudes towards European integration, in spite of so many shared policy interests, and positive reflections on the current turmoil in Europe are not easy to identify. However, it is a real achievement of the last three years that the emergence of a larger Germany has so quickly been accepted as normal.

Helen Wallace, Sussex European Institute

December 1992   Wolfgang Wessels, IEP

ACKNOWLEDGMENTS

This Chatham House Paper was prepared as part of the research activities of the European Programme of the Royal Institute of International Affairs, directed by Susie Symes. It completes work carried out by a team of researchers from both Germany and Britain – Barbara Lippert, Rosalind Stevens-Ströhmann, Dirk Günther, Grit Viertel, and Stephen Woolcock – working under Helen Wallace, former Director of the RIIA's European Programme and now Director of the Sussex European Institute at the University of Sussex, and Wolfgang Wessels, Director of the Institut für Europäische Politik in Bonn.

For this English version we owe a special vote of thanks to Margaret May, from the Publications Department of the RIIA, who in effect became one of the project team in order to edit the final publication. A longer German edition entitled *Die EG und die neuen Bundesländer – Eine Erfolgsgeschichte von kurzer Dauer? Deutsch-britische Perspektiven*, is being published simultaneously by Europa Union Verlag GmbH, Bonn for the IEP.

In producing these two editions we owe a great deal to all those who took time to meet us during the course of the project, or who attended conferences or study groups. We are particularly grateful to all those from the five new German Länder, as well as British, German and European Commission officials, members of the European Parliament and others, whose participation gave us a direct insight into developments as they took place, and the many, especially Geoffrey Edwards, whose comments on draft papers were of immense value. The responsibility for the text, however, remains with the authors.

Acknowledgments

The project was made possible by the generous support of the Anglo-German Foundation for the study of Industrial Society. In addition, the Commission of the EC in Brussels, Deutsche Bank, Land Brandenburg, the German Ministry of Foreign Affairs and the Gatsby Charitable Foundation have all given generous assistance that underpinned seminars in London and a conference in Potsdam.

January 1993   BL, RS-S, DG, GV, SW

1

INTRODUCTION

It is easy to lose sight of just what an exceptional political event German unification was. Not only because it happened at all, but because the unified Germany has remained within the European Community and NATO. In the mid-1980s such a scenario would have been seen as, at the very least, optimistic. The existence of two German states, the Federal Republic of Germany (FRG) and the German Democratic Republic (GDR), had been a symbol of a postwar status quo in Europe which had itself largely determined and been determined by the East–West conflict. For many the existence of a divided Germany was seen as a stabilizing factor, even if these views were not openly expressed. As late as June 1989 few people would have believed that unification would occur so quickly, let alone in the manner that it did. German unification must therefore be associated with major systemic change in European politics.

This study looks at one aspect of this catalyst of change, namely its interaction with the European integration process. If German unification represents systemic change, what can be said about the responses to such change? This volume analyses the German and British responses in the context of the EC. It summarizes the results of research conducted during 1990 and 1991, during the unification process, although where there have been important developments during 1992 more recent information is included. The volume considers three general questions:

(1) *What role did the EC play in the process of unification and what impact will it have in future on the economic, social and political development of the unified Germany and especially on the five new Länder?* Did the Community respond adequately to the challenge

1

posed by what was in effect an 'enlargement without accession' to the Community? How much real influence does the EC have over the process of structural adjustment still taking place in eastern Germany?

(2) *What was the impact of German unification on the EC and the European integration process?* The immediate response to unification was an intensification of European integration in the shape of two intergovernmental conferences (IGCs) on economic and monetary as well as political union, but has this effect been sustained? Initially, there was a belief that unification would not result in additional costs, in terms of increased taxes for the west Germans. This soon proved to be very wide of the mark. But are there similar delayed costs for the rest of the EC and, if so, what form do they take?

(3) *What was the impact on the role of Germany in the Community and the perceptions of Germany's role in other member states, particularly Britain?* Is there a – largely unspoken – fear of German dominance and, if so, is this leading to support for more integration, in order to anchor the more powerful, assertive Germany into the EC, or opposition to integration, out of fear that the EC will come to be dominated by Germany?

The role of the EC

The main role of the European Community in this context was to provide an essential part of the multilateral framework within which unification could occur. There can be no doubt that without the existence of the Community the issues would have been very different; indeed, unification might never have been brought about and certainly not in the way it was. The FRG's partners in the EC held to what had become part of the agreed *acquis politique* in the Community and supported unification when it rushed onto the agenda in early 1990, but they were more passive than active supporters, and the EC played a limited part in discussions during the early stages of the process. In some respects the United States was more forthright in its support of unification than some EC member states, because it was not affected by the long shadow of potential German domination.

The initial phase of unification focused on the external dimensions, popularly known in Bonn at the time as 'Neisse, NATO and neighbours': namely, the Polish border question; the question of which alliance the united Germany would belong to; upper limits on German troop levels; and questions relating to Berlin and the responsibilities and status of the four powers. These issues will be looked at in greater detail in Chapter 2, which provides a brief history of the unification process, particularly in the context of the EC. Within this context, Chapter 3 examines the pressure for institutional change in the European Parliament arising from the urgent question of representation for the east German population.

Although there was common ground between Bonn and the European Commission on the treatment of the GDR within the Community, the EC played only a limited role in the pace and nature of unification, which were dictated by the debate on so-called 'external aspects' and intra-German decisions taken in Bonn. It was Bonn that decided to offer economic, monetary and social union (GEMSU) to the GDR, in an attempt to stem the alarming flow of migrants from east to west. Bonn also determined the modalities of German monetary union, which resulted in east German industry being exposed to the full force of western competition from 1 July 1990. The EC had little or no input into these decisions even though both were to have important consequences for the whole of the Community. These macroeconomic issues are explored in Chapter 4.

Even in the areas in which Community competence was well established – in competition and regulatory policy or common commercial policy – the role of the EC was circumscribed during some of the most critical months. As Chapter 5 shows, in competition policy neither the EC nor the national authorities had any influence over the series of mergers and collaboration agreements concluded before unification on 3 October 1990. The four case-studies (Chapters 6–9) suggest that the concept of *Ordnungspolitik*,* which had been a tenet of the FRG's approach to industrial and regulatory policy, at least since the law on growth and price stability in 1969, proved to be flexible when it came to dealing with the industrial and adjustment problems in eastern Germany. The same could be said to hold for the EC's competition policy regime, for example vis-à-vis the role of the Treuhandanstalt.

In bilateral negotiations with Moscow, Bonn also made commitments early on to fulfil the GDR's outstanding contracts and obligations. This effectively pre-empted EC policies in some areas. These external political implications of unification are analysed in Chapter 10.

---

*A framework of laws based on competition rather than any form of discretionary interventionist industrial policy.

The impact on the EC

The impact of unification on the EC was more profound, especially in the short term. Prior to the opening of the Berlin Wall, economic pragmatism prevailed over political imperative in the discussion of European economic and monetary union (EMU). But unification injected a strong dose of political imperative into both GEMSU and EMU and resulted in the addition of a second IGC on political union, to include the creation of a common foreign and security policy (CFSP), more powers for the European Parliament and more majority voting. Almost immediately, however, economic pragmatism began to force its way back onto the agenda and the impetus of unification in the European integration process began to fade as other issues, such as the Gulf war and the slowing of the world and European economies, came to the fore.

With hindsight it can be argued that there was a conspiracy of optimism about the real economic costs of unification. It was felt more convenient to argue that the outcome of such an unprecedented event was uncertain rather than ask searching questions about what it would cost for each sector of the economy or interest group. The inability of the east German *Kombinate* to compete was followed by an almost total economic collapse requiring massive financial transfers from west Germany. This created inflationary pressures in west Germany and thus pressures on the Bundesbank to raise interest rates. This led, along with other factors, to upward pressure on European interest rates generally at a bad time for many countries. By 1992 many of the businesses going bankrupt or the workers laid off during the recession were finally aware of these knock-on costs of German unification. Sterling and the lira were obliged to leave the European exchange-rate mechanism (ERM). In Britain this in turn upset the political balance within the Conservative party, giving opponents of ratification of the Maastricht Treaty the advantage. In other words, unification impacted upon the rest of Europe, both economically and politically, through its impact on Germany as a whole.

This was also the case with regard to microeconomic or structural factors within Germany. During 1990, private sector actions in many cases led the way on unification before there were any legal instruments in place to regulate market structures. These actions effectively extended the west German industrial structure to the eastern Länder. The question is whether these structures will be compatible with German and EC concepts of market order. Chapter 5 examines this issue, as well as asking whether the German social market economy can survive the shock of unification.

In the short to medium term the main impact of unification has undoubtedly been on the macroeconomic parameters of the German economy. The net effect has been to weaken it through the massive increase in fiscal outgoings and the creation of inflationary pressure. But what of the longer term? If the task of transforming the east German economy can be completed, Germany could again become a motor for European economic growth. Germany's historical trading links with central and eastern Europe (examined in Chapter 10) will also have been re-established. If this happens the structural contours of the unified German economy, which were shaped during the unification process, may prove to be important. These longer-term structural issues are discussed in the case-studies. West German, as opposed to EC, influences have been particularly noticeable in financial services (Chapter 6) and the energy sector (Chapter 8). The restructuring of agriculture (Chapter 7) is a more complex issue, since it involved adjustment to the demands of the EC's Common Agricultural Policy. Chapter 9 examines shipbuilding, one of the GDR's key industrial sectors.

The impact on the role of Germany and Britain in the EC

There was a clear difference between the general approaches of the British and German governments to unification and the widespread uncertainty created by political reform in eastern Europe. In the following chapters the distinction is made between two schools of thought, as established in analytical approaches to international relations, which influenced thinking on responses to German unification. These are the *integrationist* and *realist* schools of thought.

Broadly speaking, the integrationist school of thought sees joint action and, above all, the creation of common institutions and supranational decision-making as a means of responding to political and economic challenges. Thus faced with the political and economic turmoil in central and eastern Europe, and its impact on the core of the EC through German unification, the integrationist response was to press for deepening of the Community in order to anchor Germany in the EC and to provide a pole of stability for Europe.

Adherents of the realist school are sceptical about the benefits of common institutional and legal structures in containing what are seen to be the inevitable tendencies of nation states to defend and promote their own national interest. The realist policy response to German unification, or indeed any other systemic change in the politics of the continent, therefore draws on the concepts of the balance of power and zero-sum games. The realist would argue that unification strengthens Germany; consequently any irreversible commitments to greater integration of a European Community in which a strong confident Germany would play a dominant role should be avoided at all costs. The pure balance-of-power argument would call for strong ties with allies, such as the United States, in order to redress any possible imbalance within Europe.

When the Berlin Wall was breached on 9 November 1989 the government in Bonn was as surprised as everyone else and had no strategy for how to proceed, but it quickly moved to take the political initiative. One of its top priorities was to ensure that the unified Germany would be anchored in a multilateral framework – primarily the EC and NATO. As such it was implementing long-established German policy, seeking to reassure its neighbours and to ensure that Germany would not be forced to act alone in response to challenges from the east. The approach that emerged, therefore – perhaps inevitably – owed much to the integrationist school of thought.

The British government under Margaret Thatcher shared the desire for the unified Germany to be a member of NATO. Significant further integration within the EC was, however, too high a price to pay for anchoring Germany into the west. Britain tended to be sceptical about the value of institutions and treaties in ordering relations between states. In any case there was in the government of the time an instinctive leaning towards NATO and the United States as the guarantors of European security and stability and away from European responses. In other words, the British approach to German unification seems nearer to the realist school of thought. The contrast between these two approaches is discussed further in Chapter 11.

Once the initial excitement of unification had died down and after a change of government in Britain, there were some signs of convergence in British and German policies on various aspects of EC policy – in part, at least, as a result of unification. This was, for example, the case with regard to EMU. As the costs of monetary union without economic convergence in Germany became only too apparent during 1991, the Bundesbank and others in the internal German debate who favoured a judicious approach to EMU based on purely economic considerations regained the upper hand over those who argued the case for union on political grounds, such as the Ministry of Foreign Affairs. But, as Chapter 11 concludes, the prospect of 'tactical' convergences between Britain and Germany should not disguise the fact that in the long run each government continues to hold very different views on the *finalités*, or goals, of the Community. Germany still supports European Union and a single European currency, albeit on certain specific conditions. Its approach is still strongly influenced by an integrationist turn of mind, even though doubts about the Maastricht Treaty have also been voiced within Germany. In contrast, Britain's response to the challenge of German unification and to ratification of the Maastricht Treaty shows that its approach to Europe is still strongly influenced by the realists.

2
THE HISTORY OF THE UNIFICATION PROCESS

Historically, the 'German question' in the sense of the ultimate goal of unification was always treated at one remove from the European Community and European Political Cooperation (EPC) in particular. The Federal Republic, for its part, had traditionally handled unification as a *domaine reservée*, and not as an integral part of its European policy. Support for unification from the FRG's EC partners was implicit rather than active, and there was no formal statement in EPC or the European Council acknowledging the right of the German people to self-determination and the goal of unity until November 1989. Such formal declarations as existed came under the NATO framework and numerous bilateral and joint declarations of NATO and EC members with the FRG. Nevertheless, Germany's right to self-determination had long formed part of the normative *acquis politique*. Moreover the three allied powers, France, Britain and the USA, were bound by Article 7(2) of the 1954 Treaty on Germany to accept 'a re-unified Germany enjoying a liberal-democratic constitution' and a Germany 'integrated within the European Community' (here meaning the more general community of European nations).

The legal position

The status of east Germany in the treaties establishing the Community was important when it came to considering how unification should be handled. Although the EC and its member states had conducted normal bilateral relations with the GDR since the *Grundlagenvertrag* (Basic Treaty) of 1972, they respected the special nature of the German–German relationship. This found expression in the EEC Treaty in three forms: first, in the 'Protocol on intra-German trade', according to which the exchange of goods between the FRG and the former GDR was duty- and tariff-free; second, in the 'Joint Declaration on Berlin' and the 'applicability of the Treaty of Rome in Berlin'; and, third, in the declaration by the FRG on the definition of 'German citizenship' attached to the treaty.[1] The Treaty of Rome also included special provisions allowing state aid in areas requiring special assistance as a result of the partition of Germany. A further factor was the unilateral declaration made by the FRG upon signing the Treaty of Rome that 'the Federal Republic assumes that a re-evaluation of the Treaties on the EEC and EURATOM would be a possibility in the event of unification'.[2] The possibility of using this declaration as a revision clause had long been the subject of legal and political debate in the FRG, but during 1989 and 1990 the federal government neither considered it nor threatened to use it as such. The predominant view was that unification should occur without a change in the treaties. The Commission, in the form of its President, Jacques Delors, was also of the opinion that the treatment of the GDR in the treaties suggested that its accession should be handled as a special case.[3]

Governments of all parties in the FRG have traditionally taken care to ensure that progress towards EC integration kept in step with developments in inner-German relations and in particular measures on humanitarian issues resulting from the division of Germany. In the Basic Law of the FRG the aims of '[protecting] national and state unity and [serving] world peace as an equal partner in a united Europe' are given equal weight.[4] But this did not prevent fears, across the political spectrum, that the loss of sovereignty resulting from the Single European Act, especially with regard to promoting EPC as a step towards a common foreign policy, would impose limitations on Bonn's *Deutschlandpolitik*.

The quiet, passive solidarity of the EC member states with Bonn's policy on inner-German relations was therefore only to a limited degree based on legal and political guarantees. Brussels supported Bonn in its notorious battles with the Council for Mutual Economic Assistance (CMEA) over the inclusion of Berlin (West) as part of the FRG, and thus the EC, in any international agreements, but the FRG had to force formal backing for unification out of its EC partners. Bonn could not simply rely on the assumption that support would be automatic on the basis of a given *acquis politique* or *acquis communautaire*.

The re-emergence of the German question

The transformation of eastern and central Europe and the opening of the Wall

Despite the events of 1989 and the reorientation of the smaller European CMEA states towards western Europe, the GDR under Honecker's Socialist Unity Party of Germany (SED) sought to insulate itself from the political dynamic of change. But the SED regime could neither dampen the reform which threatened to isolate it within its own socialist community of states ('Socialism in the colours of the GDR'), nor prevent the growth of domestic opposition. At the time, however, observers in Bonn and other western capitals persisted in assuming that the SED would continue to control the GDR, despite the weekly demonstrations in Leipzig during the autumn and the surge of refugees into FRG embassies in Budapest, Prague and Warsaw.

In their *nachholende Revolution*, the east Germans articulated their 'wish to catch up with Europe'. Constitutionally, this meant catching up with the legacy of bourgeois revolutions. Socially, it meant catching up with the patterns of communication and lifestyle of developed capitalism as embodied in the EC.[5] The beginning of the end of the separate existence of two German states came with the breaching of the Berlin Wall on 9 November 1989 and the practical experience of freedom of movement by the east German population. In October 1989 Willy Brandt had indicated to the German Bundestag that the most important aspects of the policy of 'small steps', introduced during his term as Chancellor, had indeed survived, at least as a German political concept. On 10 November he gave the newly emerging era of Germany its motto: 'That which belongs together will now grow together'.

The FRG's response

In those early days of November 1989 the reaction of most politicians and the media in the FRG was to stick scrupulously to the line that unification was not yet on the cards.[6] The east Germans were thought to want self-determination and freedom, but not national unity.[7] The reluctance to contemplate unification reflected an awareness of the sensitivities of Germany's partners,[8] but more importantly it reflected concerns and disorientation in the FRG about the sudden impact of the German question on Germany itself. By the end of November 1989 it was already clear that unification would be an issue in the Landtag and Bundestag elections scheduled for 1990. Equally, these elections would influence the behaviour

10

of the parties and groups within the Bundestag on the issue of unification. Chancellor Helmut Kohl felt that in these circumstances he could not allow things simply to evolve. He had to gain the political initiative on unification and sought to do so by launching his 10-Point Plan of 28 November 1989 on an unsuspecting Bundestag and indeed world – a move that precluded prior consultations with others, even the *Auswärtiges Amt* (west German Ministry of Foreign Affairs), and thus risked upsetting Germany's partners.

In practice the step-by-step approach set out in Kohl's 10-Point Plan was in accordance with Bonn's established policy on German–German relations and their place in European policy. The 're-establishment of a unified state' was referred to only as a long-term objective and then as point ten. The plan emphasized 'an organic development which took into account the interests of all parties and paved the way for a peaceful and free Europe'. The real message was that the medium-term aim should be to develop a 'confederative structure between both German states': 'that means a federal order for Germany'. Nevertheless Germany's partners noted that Kohl had omitted to include the standard undertaking of Germany's 'unshakable ties with the west'.[9] Douglas Hurd, the British Foreign Secretary, observed there was no 'eleventh point' addressing the worries and fears of Germany's partners regarding the future stability and balance of Europe. France was upset that it was not consulted beforehand and also disturbed by the absence of any reference to the German–Polish border issue (see below).

After the Wall was opened, Bonn felt an urgent need to act to stem the flood of migrants moving from east to west, which had rapidly swollen to some 1,500 a day. It also used the migration issue to solicit support among its EC partners for speedy unification, at least until the basic decision in favour of German economic and monetary union had been taken. In the east the slogans used in public demonstrations changed from 'we are the people' to 'we are *one* people', and enthusiastic popular discussion about the material aspects of reunification (such as the Deutschmark and equal and speedy access to the fruits of the social market economy) soon pushed abstract ideas about confederation or the *Vertragsgemeinschaften* (community based on treaty) off the agenda. The FRG government opted for speedy unification under Article 23 of the Basic Law (which allowed for expansion of the existing territory of the FRG). By early 1990 the *Auswärtiges Amt* working group on unification was proceeding on the premise that the provisions of Article 15 of the 1978 Vienna Convention on state successions would apply. This meant

11

that the FRG would remain the subject in international law and that both FRG and EC law would apply in the 'extended part' of the country. The European Commission's legal service doubted, however, whether this interpretation applied to a supranational organization such as the EC, believing that some EC Treaty changes might still be necessary.

The key elements of the FRG strategy that emerged in spring 1989 were as follows:

(1) a 'diffusion of German power'[10] through an EC strengthened by political union and economic and currency union;
(2) wider European cooperation through the early convening of a second Helsinki summit and the institutionalization of the Conference on Security and Cooperation in Europe (CSCE) process;
(3) the promotion of a pan-European security framework which would be created by a reform of NATO and disarmament treaties under the umbrella of CSCE;
(4) the consolidation of German–Soviet relations through a treaty on 'good neighbourliness, partnership and cooperation' (9 November 1990), which would be followed by a new generation of treaties with the countries of the former Warsaw Pact, as well as a German commitment to promote an active EC *Ostpolitik*.

Bonn was conscious of a widespread view among its EC partners, at least in 1989–90, that Germany stood to gain most from the upheavals in central and eastern Europe, and not just because of unification. Significant efforts were therefore made to present unification as part of a European process. Kohl spoke of 'Europe – [as the] future for all Germans'[11] and the Foreign Minister, Hans-Dietrich Genscher, continued to quote Thomas Mann's famous dictum: 'We want a European Germany and not a German Europe'.[12]

The EC's response
Bonn's interest in the immediate aftermath of the opening of the Wall was to keep unification as a *domaine reservée*, at least until it had its own clear strategy on how to proceed. Stressing its established policy that the division of Germany could only be removed if the division of Europe were also removed was one way of achieving this. At the informal meeting of the European Council called by President François Mitterrand in Paris on 18 November 1989, Kohl again gave assurances that European integration would be a constituent part of the Federal Republic's

raison d'être.[13] The meeting discussed the upheaval in central and eastern Europe but there was no formal agenda including German unification. At this meeting the reaction of both the British Prime Minister, Margaret Thatcher, and the Dutch Prime Minister, Ruud Lubbers, to the prospect of unification was visibly cool. Portugal and Greece quite explicitly expressed their concerns about the financial implications, while Spain, Belgium and Luxembourg were very sympathetic about the course of events in Germany.[14] But the prevailing euphoria helped Bonn to present unification as part of a wider revolution in central and eastern Europe. Indeed even Mrs Thatcher saw things in this way and spoke of 'a victory for freedom'.

At the Strasbourg European Council meeting on 8 December 1989 the Heads of State and Government adopted a carefully worded passage on German policy, but only as part of their statement on central and eastern Europe:

> We seek the strengthening of the state of peace in Europe in which the German people will regain its unity through free self-determination. This process should take place peacefully and democratically, in full respect of the relevant agreements and treaties and of all the principles defined by the Helsinki Final Act, in a context of dialogue and East–West cooperation. It also has to be placed in the perspective of European integration.[15]

This declaration served as the EC's basic policy position on the external dimension of German unification. Rather than providing a *carte blanche*, it set out a route to unification that was subject to a number of important conditions.

The *Commission* formulated a strategy at a very early stage and was in some respects ahead of the member states. President Delors, in a speech in Bruges on 17 October 1989, presented the view that the Germans' right to self-determination could not be withheld. He saw unification taking place together with a form of strengthened federalism within the EC binding the Germans permanently through European integration.[16] As early as 10/11 November, the Commission came to the view that relations between the EC and the GDR were a 'special case', possibly requiring a special enlargement via Article 23 of the Basic Law. This would avoid long and tedious treaty changes and ratification procedures. In his speech on 17 January 1990 Delors offered the GDR three routes into the Community: association, membership, or inclusion through unification with the Federal Republic. This went beyond the EC's *acquis politique* on unification at the time and left certain heads of state some way behind. For example, Mrs Thatcher was still talking more about association agreements with Poland, Hungary and the GDR.[17] Having established its position, the Commission then sought, with some success, to have it adopted as the Community position. It also pushed through the negotiations on trade and cooperation agreements with the GDR, as with other CMEA countries.[18] On 23 November 1989 the European Parliament passed a resolution on current events in East and Central Europe, supporting the right of the east Germans to become part of a united Germany and a united Europe.

The position in the *Council of Ministers* was less clear-cut. On 22 January 1990 the foreign ministers reached a common position on the methods of integration, but France, Britain and the Netherlands sought further clarification, principally on the question of 'special treatment' for a GDR accession. It took another month of bilateral discussions between the German Foreign Minister and the other member states, in which Genscher promised to provide information and give them a right to participate in the unification process, before the Commission obtained a mandate from the Council to prepare a position paper on the EC and German unification for the forthcoming special summit in Dublin. Bonn lobbied vigorously for the Article 23 option, and no change to the EC Treaty. This option was ultimately adopted by the European Council in Dublin in April 1990.

The *European Parliament* was, however, unhappy about this option: its optimal solution would have been to give its consent to the GDR's accession as a state in its own right according to the provisions of Article 237 (EEC), and it argued that for a case of 'enlargement without accession' at least some form of special decision-making mechanism would have to be established. Moreover, the Commission concluded in April 1990 that work in other areas, such as the internal market programme, should not be delayed by what were potentially lengthy processes of treaty changes and the ratification of these by national parliaments. This necessitated the integration of the GDR with no institutional changes. The FRG was taken at its word that it would not seek such changes, particularly in representation. This issue is discussed further in Chapter 3.

The British response

Britain, with its special responsibility for Berlin and Germany as a whole as a result of its role as one of the four wartime allied powers, regarded the German question primarily as a question of European security. The initial British response to unification focused on two main preoccupations: first, how could the existing European security structures be adapted to the changes that German unification would bring about, and what impact would unification have on Germany's role in NATO and the politico-military status of the USSR; and second, would Germany become more powerful and pose a threat to its neighbours? The British objective was also to bind a democratic unified Germany within a solid European security system composed of NATO as well as Western European Union (WEU). A neutral Germany would not have been acceptable for the British government, which also emphasized the overriding need for the retention of a US military and security policy presence in the 'new Europe'.

British opinion on the 'German question' during 1990 fell into three general categories. The first is what might be called the 'Königswinter' category, although this extended beyond the participants of the Königswinter conferences and included other similarly well-informed Anglo-German circles. This category of opinion saw the opening of the Wall as a signal of a welcome 'normalization' of Germany and one which should contribute to European stability. Normalization meant a unified Germany assuming full sovereign rights and responsibilities within both EC and international law.

The second category found expression in official government policy which adhered to the 'realist' school of thought, favouring prudent and circumspect international and EC policies which could bind the unified Germany into the western security and economic structures.

The third category of opinion reflected a concern about or even mistrust of a unified and thus strengthened Germany. This was accompanied by a strong antipathy towards European integration which precluded strategies based on 'containing' Germany within a more integrated EC. This opinion was predominantly held by certain (mostly Conservative) politicians of the generation that had experienced the Second World War and found its most notorious expression in an interview with a cabinet minister, Nicholas Ridley, published in the *Spectator*.[19] It was felt in some quarters that Ridley had in fact been expressing Mrs Thatcher's personal views, but if this was the case they were not reflected in her official statements, and general public opinion at the time was, if anything, towards the opposite (positive) end of the spectrum.

On 24 March, one week before the Königswinter meeting, Mrs Thatcher invited six authorities on the history and politics of Germany to

Chequers, her official country home, to hear their views on the international role of a united Germany. According to a memorandum attributed to Charles Powell, the Prime Minister's private secretary, a list of the less flattering characteristics of the German character was discussed, such as '*Angst*, aggressiveness, assertiveness, bullying, egotism, inferiority complex, sentimentality'.[20] But the overriding view of the group was that Germany's postwar record suggested that it could be trusted. Interestingly, the Chequers meeting did not really discuss the EC or economic dimensions of unification and there was no one present with obvious EC credentials.

It was not so much the substance of the Chequers discussions which was found disturbing in Germany, but the style of the British debate and the fact that important figures close to Mrs Thatcher, if not the Prime Minister herself, hovered between the 'official' and more extreme viewpoints on unification, even if both the media and mainstream public opinion were far more sanguine. Bonn therefore preferred to hear the official, 'unification-friendly', governmental position and chose to regard the controversy over Ridley's statement, which led to his resignation as Secretary of State for Trade and Industry, as an internal affair.

The initial emphasis on security concerns did not mean that the British government was not also active in other aspects of German unification. At the end of January the Foreign and Commonwealth Office (FCO) started to examine other aspects, and from February Whitehall was busy with a detailed legal and technical analysis of the impact of German unification. One consequence of this was that Britain was better prepared than any of Germany's other EC partners for the negotiations on legal adjustments over the GDR's 'accession' to the EC. Britain was also the only partner to send a delegation to discuss the details with the federal Ministry of Economics in Bonn.

Franco-German relations

The German question has always loomed larged in the postwar history of French–German relations. On the one hand, France has been constantly on its guard for any signs of a loosening of the FRG's *Westbindung* (western ties), or of a diminution of its commitment to the west European integration process. On the other hand, Franco-German reconciliation was one of the principal foundations of the EC, and the *entente élémentaire*[21] has been a cornerstone of both German and French European policy. France was therefore anxious to ensure that German unification did not devalue this privileged relationship. These preoccupations were reflected in the diverse French responses to the events of November 1989. Fears that Germany might become an *économie dominante* were soon replaced by a concern about the knock-on effects of German economic *weakness*. France, in contrast to Britain, saw strengthening the EC as a means of tying Germany more closely to the future of Europe.

The French believed that a rapid unification might not only endanger the already fragile state of the Gorbachev reform process in the USSR, but also the balance of Europe. The qualified support for unification in the Strasbourg European Council communiqué therefore reflected French, as well as British, concerns. In his 1990 new year speech, Mitterrand replied indirectly to Kohl's 10-Point Plan by proposing a confederation encompassing the whole of Europe; once again he signalled the need for German and European unification to go hand in hand.

For Germany, too, it was very important to ensure that unification did not jeopardize the Franco-German relationship and that France adopted a supportive position. Initial French doubts therefore precipitated a redoubling of efforts on the part of Bonn. The improvement in relations was underlined in a speech by Kohl in Paris on 17 January, in which he outlined his government's position on the Polish border issue and on the 10-Point Plan, and repudiated accusations that the plan represented a timetable that would force the pace of unification. He also emphasized the importance of close cooperation between Bonn and Paris in their efforts to deepen European integration. The French response to the results of the east German Volkskammer elections in March was to go for an acceleration of European integration to tie Germany into the EC. According to the Chancellor's adviser, Horst Teltschik,[22] from that point on both German and French officials worked flat out to integrate the initiatives on German unification and European integration. They paved the way for the joint letter from Kohl and Mitterrand to EC member states on 14 April,[23] proposing a faster timetable for economic and monetary union and the addition of a second intergovernmental conference on political union.

The security dimension: the 2+4 negotiations
In early 1990 there emerged three different dimensions to the debate on unification, each of which had its respective negotiating forum: first, the *external dimension*, for which a '2+4' framework was established in Ottawa; second, the *internal German dimension*, for which the Cabinet Committee for German Unity was established in Bonn to handle the

contractual arrangements with the GDR for GEMSU; and finally, the *EC dimension*, which was discussed in the special 'German unity' working groups of Commission and Parliament and in the Council of EC Foreign Ministers, and a special meeting of the European Council was envisaged.

Between the opening of the Wall and the signing in Moscow of the treaty on Germany in September 1990, it was the security dimension which attracted the greatest interest among governments and in public debate. This period can be divided in three: from Malta to Moscow; from Ottawa to the first 2+4 ministerial meeting; and the breakthrough in Moscow and its confirmation in Paris.

From Malta to Moscow

The outlines of how a unified Germany would fit into the new European order were set between the Malta summit of 2/3 December 1989, at which Presidents Bush and Gorbachev announced the end of the cold war, and the Moscow meeting in February 1990 between Gorbachev and Kohl and their foreign ministers Eduard Shevardnadze and Genscher. During this time one of the great unknowns was the position of the USSR. Both Britain and France argued that it was important to consider the consequences of a rapid or ill-prepared unification for Gorbachev. Mitterrand recounted Gorbachev's concern that 'German reunification would be followed by a two-lined announcement after which a Marshall would assume my office'.[24] Mrs Thatcher appeared on occasions as the guardian of the USSR;[25] this was seen as somewhat ironical in Bonn, which had long hoped for a concrete contribution from London to *Ostpolitik*. The reality was that the USSR was seeking a new role as its empire collapsed, and partnership with the West, not least with the FRG, was an important element of this. As one of the four powers and as the power behind the Warsaw Pact and the CMEA in which the GDR had once been a junior but key partner, the USSR had clear responsibilities in the debate on unification, but its response to the fall of the Berlin Wall showed no clear policy towards Germany. Indeed it remained unclear how much 'old-style' thinking on Germany had survived the declared end of the cold war. This uncertainty was reflected in Shevardnadze's speech to the Political Committee of the European Parliament on 19 December 1989,[26] although the speech did make clear that the USSR wished to deal with the German question in the widest possible European context, especially within the CSCE process.

In addition to dealing with the USSR, a negotiating framework had to be found that would incorporate the status of the western allies as joint members of the four-power group and nuclear powers, as well as accommodate the NATO and WEU guarantees needed for stability. 'Neisse, NATO and neighbours'[27] soon emerged as the three key issues in the external debate. Moreover the FRG kept the circle of negotiating partners relatively small and 'neutralized' the influence of the GDR government in areas in which the latter had its own ideas. On most other issues related to unification the GDR mainly played a supporting role to that of Bonn.

There were some difficult moments over the handling of the four-power issue. On 11 December 1989 the ambassadors of the four powers met in Berlin for the first time in 18 years, supposedly to discuss the situation in the GDR. Gorbachev had proposed the talks as a means of revitalizing the four-power responsibilities and because of his avowed wish to consult with Bush, Mitterrand and Thatcher. For Bonn it was of vital importance to be associated with any discussions or negotiations about Germany, as it had been since Geneva (1958) in meetings with the three western allies through the so-called Bonn Group. Consequently Bonn stressed that the four-power meeting in Berlin required 'considerable explanation'. The supportive role of the United States was important for the Bonn government. In his visit to Berlin earlier that month, Secretary of State Baker had gone out of his way to emphasize that the USA stood by its unwavering support for German unification which it had reaffirmed even as the Berlin Wall was being breached on the night of 9 November. In contrast to the Europeans, the Americans were not distracted by concerns about a unified Germany coming to dominate Europe economically or politically. By May 1990 President Bush was offering Germany 'an equal partnership in leadership', which would be all the more important with a united Germany.[28] With the end of East–West conflict, US security policy towards Europe was in need of a new focus, and the unifying Germany became this focus.

The *German–Polish border issue* was not well handled by Bonn. The absence of a binding guarantee of the Polish border under international law had damaged relations between Bonn and Warsaw for decades and had nurtured speculation about Germany's 'revisionist' ambitions even among its western partners. Quite coincidentally, the close link between the German question and the German–Polish relationship was highlighted by the fact that Chancellor Kohl was visiting Poland when the Wall was breached. The very previous day, Kohl's Warsaw interlocutors, including Walesa, Mazowiecki and Jaruzelski, had expressed their concerns about what would happen if the SED state collapsed and a powerful Germany re-emerged. Concerns about the border issue were not limited to Poland. In its resolution of 23 November 1989, the European Parliament called for a guarantee of Poland's western border. France's angry reaction to the 10-Point Plan was also, in part, due to the absence of any such guarantee, which was also stressed, for example, by the second chamber of the Netherlands parliament.

Although neither NATO nor the EC member states really believed a German government would consider any claim to territories east of the Oder–Neisse line, Bonn's refusal to give a clear undertaking to this effect led to incomprehension and irritation abroad. The government avoided a 'decisive formulation' for 'exclusively domestic and party political reasons'[29] and although Kohl held firm to this view until both the Bundestag and Volkskammer had passed a joint resolution on 21 July 1990 confirming Germany's eastern border, others, including Genscher, President von Weizsäcker, and the parliamentary opposition groups, had long been pressing for a clear confirmation by Bonn. Its failure in this respect gave credence to those who had doubts about either unification or the speed at which it was taking place. In response France proposed the inclusion of Poland in the 2+4 talks. In an interview with *Der Spiegel* in March 1990, Mrs Thatcher used the issue to raise doubts about Kohl's assurances to Warsaw and thus, implicitly, about the speed of unification.

The *Alliance issue* was better handled. Bonn was clearly very aware of sensitivities on a unified Germany's alliance membership and succeeded in striking a balance between the need to keep Moscow happy and not questioning Germany's *Westbindung*. Thus Genscher's formula at the end of January 1990 that the NATO structure should not be extended to the territory of the GDR was geared to his visit to Moscow on 10/11 February. At the same time he confirmed the *Westbindung*, rejected the concept of German neutrality, welcomed Gorbachev's suggestion for a CSCE summit, and denied the need for separate GDR membership of the EC.[30] The USA was afraid that the CSCE proposal might become a 'substitute peace negotiation' and did not agree to this idea until the resolution of the NATO Council on 7 February. The western allies agreed with the FRG that negotiations on the implications of the ever more likely unification should be held among the six. Moscow agreed to this in February after intensive talks between Baker and Gorbachev. Among the western allies differences in approach were reflected in the formula '4+2' preferred by Britain and France (which reflected a subordinate role for the FRG and GDR), while the US and FRG preferred '2+4'.[31] The '2+4' formula was adopted and the negotiations assumed the role of a sort of steering group for the international aspects of German unification.

A first breakthrough came during the visit to Moscow by Kohl and Genscher in early February 1990, when the USSR government clarified its position and effectively gave a green light for unification. Provided the USSR's interests, rights and obligations with regard to Germany were respected, Moscow said it was up to the FRG and GDR to decide on whether unification should occur, and if so, how fast. Kohl and Genscher responded generously to this position and made commitments which were, at least potentially, binding on EC and not just German policy. For example, they promised to respect existing trade agreements and contracts between the GDR and the USSR which, on the 'accession' of the GDR to the EC, would become the substance of EC commercial policy. Bonn's generosity was also shown in the provision of DM200m in food aid. The EC dimension to the undertakings made by Kohl was underlined by the fact that his first call on returning from Moscow was to Jacques Delors to inform him of the breakthrough on the 'external aspects' of unification.[32] Kohl knew he needed the greatest possible support from Brussels to get the external questions through the EC.

From Ottawa to the first 2+4 ministerial
The second phase of the debate on the external and security aspects of unification lasted from the Ottawa meeting, where the 2+4 formula was officially announced in the margins of the Open Skies Conference on 13 February, to the first 2+4 meeting at foreign minister level on 5 May 1990. The 2+4 approach was the best option for the FRG but countries excluded were less happy. Both the Netherlands and Italy demanded, without success, the right to participate, e.g. in the EPC framework. By this stage Britain supported German unity unreservedly: this was underlined by an interview with Douglas Hurd in *Die Welt*.[33] But there were still some doubts in Bonn as to whether Downing Street fully shared the official policy represented by the FCO.

The immediate task after Ottawa was to set up the 2+4 machinery. This was done at the first official-level talks in Bonn on 14 March, which also agreed an agenda covering the key issues affecting the external aspects, namely the border question (on which Poland was to be included); political and military questions, in particular united Germany's alliance membership, and the upper limit on German armed forces; questions relating to Berlin; and the four-power duties and responsibilities. The Community played no active role in these discussions on security-related issues and the topic was not covered at either of the Dublin European Council meetings, in April and June 1990. However, some exchange of information between the European Parliament and the US and Soviet negotiators took place in the 2+4 talks at the end of June.

By February 1990 the FRG government, Genscher in particular, had come to believe that it was necessary to provide Moscow with 'the script' for German unification – in other words, for initiatives to come from the West. The February meeting in Moscow had confirmed that the USSR placed the utmost importance on the question of how to deal with the two military alliances. Genscher therefore sought ways of resolving the issue. Addressing the WEU assembly in March, he spoke of German unity as a 'contribution to European security' and of the need for 'cooperative security structures', first to complement and then to replace the existing alliances.[34] He repeatedly offered variations on his theme of the non-expansion of NATO jurisdiction to the GDR. Bonn also proposed a declaration of non-aggression. NATO's response was all the more important for the USSR when it became clear that the Warsaw Pact was disintegrating. At the meeting of the Political Advisers' Committee on 7 June, Lothar de Maizière, leader of the coalition government, spoke of a 'first-class burial' for the Warsaw Pact.

Not surprisingly, it took some time for the USSR to come to terms with a unified Germany in NATO. In April it relayed its famous neutrality demand and followed this with repeated calls for Germany to belong to both NATO and the Warsaw Pact. At the foreign ministers' first 2+4 meeting the Soviets appeared more amenable to the German offer of a 'package solution.'[35] Bonn also offered a large line of credit for the USSR and a treaty-based privileged relationship between Bonn and Moscow in the form of a so-called *Generalvertrag* (general treaty).

Kohl adopted a more forthright approach to the issue of alliance membership in the run-up to the US–Soviet summit in Washington at the end of May, suggesting the so-called 'Hamlet' formula of the CSCE Final Act and UN Charter, according to which every state had the right 'to be or not to be' a member of an alliance. But despite intensive preparations the Washington summit achieved neither a breakthrough on the core issues nor clarification of Moscow's position. The intense summit diplomacy and high-level meetings continued unabated but showed signs of only gradual progress towards a rapprochement. Progress at the sixth 2+4 round on 4 July was minimal, as Soviet diplomacy continued to test Western solidarity. The NATO meeting at Turnberry on 7/8 June had ended with a clear statement on Germany's membership of NATO, but with the proviso that NATO structures would not be established on the territory of the GDR for 7 years. The crucial point was that NATO wanted to extend a hand of friendship to the USSR and the other countries of eastern Europe. The NATO special summit of 5/6 July in London proposed a declaration of non-aggression between the two pacts and provided elements of a new definition of the relationship between NATO and the Warsaw Pact or Eastern Europe. Here was the script for Gorbachev, who could now justify Soviet concessions on the issue of alliance membership to his domestic opponents. Finally, the FRG declared its readiness to make a binding commitment on an upper limit of personnel in the German armed forces.

The breakthrough in Moscow

The breakthrough on the question of NATO membership occurred during private discussions between Kohl and Gorbachev on the first day of Kohl's and Genscher's visit to Moscow from 14 to 16 July 1990. The main points of the comprehensive eight-point statement, which Kohl announced to a rather surprised public at Arkhis in the Caucasus,[36] were: (a) a free choice by the unified Germany on alliance membership, whereby the Chancellor made it clear that this would amount to NATO membership; (b) the complete dissolution of four-power rights on German unification and thus the establishment of full German sovereignty; (c) agreement of treaties on the removal of Soviet troops from GDR territory and an agreement covering the effects of the introduction of the Deutschmark into the GDR; (d) no extension of NATO structures to the territory of the GDR while Soviet troops were stationed there but immediate application of the security guarantee under Articles 6 and 7 of the NATO Treaty to the whole of German territory; (e) a unilateral commitment by the FRG to reduce the strength of its armed forces to 370,000 within three to four years. Germany was also to continue to renounce the manufacture, deployment or use of nuclear weapons. This last point was never an issue for Bonn, although there was considerable interest in Britain.

These points of agreement were endorsed at the 2+4 meeting in Paris on 17 July, in which Polish Foreign Minister Skubiszewski also took part. On 30 August Genscher delivered a commitment to a maximum of 370,000 armed forces for the united Germany, and the reductions were announced by the federal government in conjunction with the Conventional Forces in Europe (CFE) on 19 November.[37] The withdrawal of Soviet troops from the territory of the GDR is due to be completed by the end of 1994. On 12 September the 'Treaty on the Final Settlement with Respect to Germany' was signed in Moscow by the 2+4. This was ratified by the parliaments and came into force on 15 March 1991.

23

On 14 November 1990 Genscher, now as Foreign Minister of the united Germany, together with Skubiszewski, signed the treaty confirming the existing borders between Poland and Germany.[38] Five days later the 22 states of NATO and the Warsaw Pact signed a non-aggression treaty. Finally, the CSCE Charter of Paris welcomed the unification of Germany as a 'significant contribution to a lasting legal peace order for a united democratic Europe'.[39] With its representation by the Commission of the EC and the Presidency of the Council as signatories of the Charter of Paris, the Community was brought *ex post* into the agreement on the external (political) aspects of unification. But the conclusion of the external negotiations to a certain extent cleared the way for the internal discussions within the EC. As Genscher put it after praising the settlement with the USSR as a move towards the construction of a European peace order with NATO as the cornerstone, as well as an institutionalization of the CSCE process, 'it now remained to create a Political Union of the EC states'.

The German–German negotiations: where did the EC come in?

At its very first meeting (7 February 1990) the so-called 'Cabinet Committee for German Unification' decided to move to create an economic and currency union with the GDR. The election soon afterwards of the 'Alliance for Germany' (closely aligned with the CDU/CSU (West)), on 18 March, under de Maizière, was interpreted as a vote for speedy unification, the introduction of the Deutschmark and the acceptance of the west German economic and social order. This election result opened the way for GEMSU and within two days the governing coalition parties had agreed on 1 July 1990 as the target date for its realization. This date was set without consulting any of the Community bodies, even though the Community would, potentially, be significantly affected.

The responsibility for coordination of the negotiations on the *Staatsvertrag* fell to the Federal Ministry of Finance. Its chief negotiator was Hans Tietmeyer, who was also a member of the board of the Bundesbank. The negotiations were initiated by the presentation, on 24 April, of a working document by the recently elected coalition government in east Berlin. There followed four weeks of intensive negotiation. By 2 May both sides had agreed on the conversion rate for the Ostmark (see Chapter 5). By the time the *Staatsvertrag* on GEMSU was signed by the Finance Ministers Waigel (FRG) and Romberg (GDR), on 18 May 1990, the west German ruling parties had agreed to hold all-German elections in place of the scheduled Bundestag elections. This gave new impetus to the unification process, in which the domestic and international dimensions were synchronized. It was not until May that a 'parliamentary dimension' of the decision-making process was introduced. This allowed only a month for agreement on the *Staatsvertrag* to be reached by the Bundesrat (the west German upper house) and the Bundestag. A Bundestag Committee on German Unity was supposed to provide an input into the debate, in parallel with a similar Volkskammer committee. But as it did not convene until the day the *Staatsvertrag* was signed, it had no substantial impact on the public or official debate.

The European Parliament's complaint that it was not consulted on the *Staatsvertrag* must be seen against the background of this rather cursory consultation with even the German parliaments. During the negotiation of the *Staatsvertrag* the European Parliament was dependent on gaining information indirectly via the Commission. Kohl, responding to Delors's wish for a political gesture from Bonn in support of the Community, had briefed the Commission personally on 23 March. He advocated once more an accelerated development of the Community towards political union. Despite consultations between Commission officials and east and west German negotiators, it was clear that consultations with the EC institutions needed to be strengthened to avoid similar problems over the *Einigungsvertrag* (Treaty of Unification). Moreover, as the following chapters will show, the GEMSU agreement and the speed with which it was introduced had important implications for the whole of the EC. The Commission in its statement on the *Staatsvertrag* agreed that it was the main instrument for integrating east Germany into the economic order of the FRG and EC as well, and that it took full account of EC legislation.

Unity through accession

Responsibility for the negotiations over the unification treaty was given to the Interior Ministry. These negotiations lasted no longer than five weeks, from 6 July to 31 August, when the treaty was signed by Interior Minister Schäuble (FRG) and State Secretary Krause (GDR). The head of the Commission's task force, Carlo Trojan, took part in negotiations right from the start.

The *Einigungsvertrag* touched practically every area of the unified Germany's legal framework. As with the *Staatsvertrag*, FRG law was extended, with very few exceptions, to the unified Germany, and was thus already compatible with EC legislation. In any case, most of the material relevant to the EC had already been regulated by the *Staatsvertrag*. From the beginning the two German treaty partners worked on the basis that all treaties or agreements entered into by the old FRG under European or international law would remain in force and apply to the unified Germany, including, of course, EC membership. This was not the case with agreements entered into by the GDR, their applicability to the FRG being assessed on a case-by-case basis. Three broad criteria were used: legitimate trade expectations (*Vertrauensschutz*); the interests of the affected parties; and an assessment of the contractual obligations of the Federal Republic under the basic principles of democratic and constitutional order while 'respecting the jurisdiction of the European Community'.

Where the jurisdiction of the EC or other entities was affected, a decision of the status of treaties or agreements (whether originally concluded by the FRG or by the GDR) was reached only after consultation with the party concerned. Intra-German treaties were compatible with EC legislation and obligations.

EC management of unification

The Commission: working groups and task force

On 9 February 1990 the Commission established a special working group under Commissioner Bangemann, which focused on industrial/economic and internal aspects of unification. Shortly afterwards two further working groups were set up on external and trade policy, under Commissioner Andriessen, and financial and currency policy, under Commissioner Christophersen. Work had already begun on what adaptations of EC secondary legislation would be required. The first Commission communication for the European Council in Dublin was produced under the direction of a group of four (these three Commissioners plus Delors). A special task force on German unification under Carlo Trojan, which met for the first time on 8 May 1990, was responsible for operational and coordination arrangements, and for the legal framework for integration. It consisted of permanent representatives from Directorates General dealing with external relations, external trade, internal market, budget and structural policy. On the German side an inter-institutional group was also set up in Bonn under the joint coordination of the Foreign Ministry and the Ministry of Economic Affairs, but in practice it was the latter which prepared the first study on ways of reconciling GDR structures and practice with EC legislation. Internal ministerial contacts between Bonn and the GDR began only after the coalition government had been formed under de Maizière and were intensified after GEMSU.

The Commission also conducted its own enquiries with east Berlin, at least in those areas, such as agriculture and external trade, in which the EC had primary competence. The workload in both these areas was enormous. For example, there were some 3,000 GDR agreements on external trade, mainly with the CMEA countries, which had to be 'clarified'. The Commission thus provided an important channel of information for the other EC member states which was essential in helping them prepare for the negotiations in the Council and Committee of Permanent Representatives (COREPER).

The European Council decisions
The special meeting of the European Council in Dublin on 28 April adopted a Commission paper on unification which endorsed, in particular, the basic principle that the integration of the new Länder should proceed without any changes to the EEC Treaty. The Commission strategy as set out in this paper envisaged three phases in the process.[40]

The first, 'interim', phase began with GEMSU on 1 July 1990. From this date measures applied in the GDR to promote social and economic reform were to conform to EC standards and the Commission was to be kept continuously informed. This applied particularly to observance of competition rules (see Chapter 5), the introduction of value added tax, equal opportunities for non-German investors, as well as the establishment of a market-orientated and EC-compatible system of credit, price, taxation and social insurance systems. Although EC law did not yet apply to the GDR during this phase, Community instruments for providing credit were already deployed, and other programmes offered immediate assistance. Despite these contributions, the EC had no direct opportunity to influence key decisions affecting economic and structural conditions in the GDR before the treaty of union. During this phase, Chancellor Kohl eschewed any German demand for assistance under structural or other funds. It was clear, however, that the future need for structural adjustment in the new Länder would be likely to result in a need for EC funds.

Only in the second, so-called transitional phase, beginning with unification on 3 October, did Community law, both primary and secondary, automatically apply to the territory of the GDR. The ideal date for the final phase, by which time all the adaptation measures had to be in place, was to be 1 January 1993, the original date for completion of the internal market. The Council decided on this date in principle in December 1990, with the exception of some environmental standards.

Many of the doubts and fears of Germany's EC partners were allayed at an early stage of the negotiations. Indeed, by the time of an informal meeting of EC foreign ministers in Dublin on 21 April, most issues had been resolved. Such progress on the details of the GDR's integration into the EC cannot be seen in isolation from the broader debate about European unification. The joint Franco-German letter of 14 April represented an important breakthrough here, effectively proposing that 1990 would become the year not only of German unification, but also of European union.

By the time of the next European Council summit, in Dublin in June 1990, most of the issues concerning the formal, legal integration of the GDR had been resolved. The *Staatsvertrag* was endorsed at this meeting, and two other relevant issues were discussed: the convening of the two intergovernmental conferences, scheduled for 14 December in Rome, and the decision to offer association agreements to the GDR's immediate neighbours in the east.

The European Parliament's role
The European Parliament also concerned itself from an early stage with the effects of the unification process on the EC. On 15 February it set up an 'Ad Hoc Committee for German Unification', which was actively assisted by the Commission. It had a broad remit covering institutional, political as well as sectoral aspects of unification, and soon became the focus of the Parliament's work on unification. Direct channels of communication and consultation were established with both German states, and the Bundestag and Volkskammer were invited to participate in the Committee's deliberations. Hearings were also staged with representatives of business and sectoral associations in both east and west Germany, including the Treuhandanstalt. The Committee also gathered first-hand evidence on some crucial issues, such as agriculture, energy and the environment. The Committee met fourteen times between 1 March and its dissolution on 11 December. It produced three interim reports as well as its final report, and organized discussion of German unification in six plenary sessions of the Parliament.

The first 'Donnelly Report'
The first interim report,[41] which questioned the validity of assumption about a 'frictionless' unification, set out the aims and principles of the EC's approach: (a) unification had to be achieved in a manner consistent

28

with the aims of European integration, above all the completion of the internal market and EMU; (b) financial support for the GDR territory must not be at the expense of structurally weak regions in other parts of the EC; (c) all EC measures with respect to the GDR had to be consistent with policy towards central and eastern Europe, particularly trade relations between the CMEA countries.

The report presented the Parliament with a provisional assessment of the political, economic, legal and social effects of unification. It pointed out that the unique character of German unification concealed huge uncertainties, given that there was no experience of transforming a centrally planned economy to a market economy. On the other hand the GDR was at least the leading CMEA economy and was linked with the strongest country in the EC. Unification was seen, on balance, as beneficial for the political, economic and social conditions in the GDR. The pressure points requiring major adaptation to comply with EC rules largely corresponded with those identified by the Commission: a range of quality, health, safety and environmental standards; agricultural and fishery policies; transport and environmental policies; external trade; and structural policy. The implications for EC institutions were considered only in terms of the representation in the European Parliament of the sixteen million east Germans (see Chapter 3). There was insufficient information to estimate the financial effects accurately. On balance it seemed likely that there would be a burden on the EC budget, but not an excessive one.

The European Parliament therefore adopted a constructive, cooperative approach to its involvement in the process of consultation, assuming that the legal EC integration process would for the most part be dependent upon goodwill and informal cooperation which could limit its own involvement and strengthen the position of the Commission. It did not insist on having the right to formally ratify the integration of the GDR as an 'act of enlargement', as defined in Article 237 of the EC Treaty.

The 'Commission package' and special powers for the Commission
On 21 August the European Commission presented to the Council a catalogue of provisions adapting EC secondary legislation to accommodate adjustment in east Germany.[42] It proposed only 22 legislative measures,[43] and explicitly excluded consideration of the 'contribution of German unification to internal and external development of the Community' as well as 'the geopolitical effects on Europe as a whole'. It argued that the positive effects of unification in both areas were clear, in the first case

because there had been an acceleration of the EMU process and a second IGC on political union; and in the second because unification was helping to build a Community that could provide 'a new solid basis for peace, security and cooperation' in Europe.

The decision, taken in Bonn, to bring forward unification from 1 January 1991 to 3 October 1990 created a dilemma for the EC. The Community had envisaged the completion of its package of legislation by 31 December. There was no way that the EC could complete approval of the package by normal means before the end of 1990, but failure to do so would have created a legal vacuum during the last three months of the year. The Community and all its institutions showed considerable flexibility in overcoming this problem. On 17 July the Council approved a Commission proposal allowing itself greater powers for the three-month period to enable it to implement the legislation, on condition that such an action should not set any precedents. For its part the European Parliament agreed to handle the legislation rapidly by holding, for the first time, two readings of the legislation during the same week (11 and 13 September).

On 6 September discussions took place between the President of the Parliament, the Commission and the Council. Uniquely, the Parliament was consulted on all legislative measures, independent of any existing legal basis, and examined and approved the legislation as a package.

The Council and COREPER at the centre of decision-making

The Committee of Permanent Representatives and above all its ad hoc group on German unification dealt with the package of legislation within the record time of three months.[44] The Commission was represented on the ad hoc group by a member of the Task Force, by a legal expert and, depending on the topic, by someone from the appropriate Directorate General. The Council Secretariat provided a first point of reference for delegations with specific concerns, thus reducing the load to be dealt with in the meetings of COREPER. The GDR was only involved unofficially in the negotiations, as part of the German delegation, but officials with special expertise were sometimes consulted, especially over trade issues.

Among the most active delegations were Britain, France and Spain. The British delegation was particularly concerned about unfair competition from east Germany or the risk of goods imported duty-free into east Germany from the CMEA countries flooding the EC. Britain argued for a one-year limit on the derogation on duty-free goods, but the European Parliament's proposal of two years was eventually approved, to the relief of Poland and the Soviet Union. Bonn guaranteed that it would enforce the *Endverbleibsregelung*, which required products not conforming to EC standards to remain in the GDR, by a system of fines. This removed the case for maintaining border controls between the old and the new Länder. The Commission undertook to ensure that EC competition policy was enforced in the territory of the GDR.

The predominant view, particularly in the Commission, was that Germany would be strengthened by unification. The European Parliament, however, placed more emphasis on the uncertainties involved in the process of systemic change and its social consequences. Few, if any, of those involved in the negotiations believed at the time that unification would result in a fundamental weakening of Germany.

The outcome
On 22 November the European Parliament approved the transitional measures set out in the Commission's proposed package of legislation. On 4 December the Council approved the minor interim and adaptation measures. From 3 October some 80% of existing EC law applied in the new Länder. To the relief of the southern member states, structural fund allocations under the existing programme through to 1993 were not affected: the 3 billion ecus set aside by the Community for the five new Länder were additional funds. The EC institutions' evaluation of their own performance, as well as that of outsiders, was generally positive. The Commission felt that the efficiency, flexibility and political maturity of the Community institutions had been amply demonstrated. In its resolution of 24 October 1990 the Parliament welcomed unification 'as the greatest and in its form the most unique historical experience which contributes to the dismantling of barriers between eastern and western Europe and to the realization of a wider goal of the European Union.'[45]

Conclusions
The inner-German dynamic of *Einheit durch Beitritt* (unity through accession) was the force that led the EC and the four powers, as early as February/March 1990, to create a European framework for the rapid unification timetable, and for plans for a German *Sonderweg* (separate path) to be abandoned. A number of factors came into play: the rapid collapse of the political, institutional and economic structures in the GDR; the threat of increasing east–west migration; the desire on the part of the GDR population for immediate participation in the social market economy and in a democratic constitution; the favourable economic

climate in the FRG; the belief that a sharp shock to the political and economic system was the most effective way to modernize the GDR; election and party political considerations; the danger that the USSR might become paralysed as a result of its inner conflicts, and that Gorbachev's position would be further undermined; the fear of losing the opportunity presented by the prevailing European and international situation.

The German government took the initiatives, but the EC's cooperative stance, and its importance as a factor for political stability in Europe, as well as European integration as a 'fundamental' for unification, should not be underestimated. Unification was not just brought about by the particular leadership qualities of the main actors, particularly Kohl and Gorbachev. The Community's low-key approach was in keeping with the 'continuity' of Germany's EC policy. The EC sought to normalize the situation as quickly as possible, with equal treatment for the new Länder, rather than to treat Germany as a special case. The response of EC institutions reflected their concern to show flexibility and political maturity, and not to let unification founder over relatively trivial issues. Both the EC and the German government banked on the force of 'integrationism', presenting positive scenarios for the rapid social and economic transformation of the new Länder. The real test for this strategy was postponed until 1991 and the Maastricht agreement, but in the interim Germany came to be perceived generally as 'strong' rather than 'weak' – a perception that persists in Europe, despite the recent economic upheavals.

3

THE QUESTION OF REPRESENTATION IN THE EUROPEAN PARLIAMENT

It was always a fundamental aim of the FRG to bring about German unification within the framework of European integration, primarily to reassure its EC partners and to keep their trust. In order to make the process as painless and unobtrusive as possible for the other member states, the negotiations were, right from the start, to involve no change to the EC treaties.[1] It was made clear that the FRG would not seek alterations to the EC institutions as a result of the incorporation of the new Länder and would thereby avoid any shifts in the balance of power within the decision-making mechanism of the Community. German unification did not change the number of Commissioners, the number of judges in the European Court of Justice or voting weights in the Council. Nevertheless the European Parliament (EP) itself raised the question of how the sixteen million additional citizens were to be represented until the next general elections in 1994.

In the beginning the GDR expressed its own ideas about representation within the Community bodies for the interim period until full German unification: it wished to have observer status in the Community groups and also in negotiations on unification at the European level. The GDR's Minister for Foreign Affairs at that time wanted to include the question of the number of MEPs from East Germany in the negotiations with the EC. Likewise, the second German Commissioner was to come from the GDR. These demands were to have been part of the negotiations over the unification treaty but were later dropped by the GDR government, because the federal government pursued a different strategy.

Representation up to 1994 – interim arrangements

The EP's Legal Committee, concerned to avoid any lack of democracy, demanded in an Opinion to the Special Committee for German Unification[2] that a precedent be set by providing a special observer status for representatives of the GDR, which was to apply until the next elections to the EP. Meanwhile a considered, long-term solution was to be found for future representation. To secure this special observer status, a change to EP procedures was required, which was opposed by the French and British, and to a lesser extent also by Spanish, Portuguese and Italian MEPs.

The Christian Democrat Group in the EP became actively involved in this question and on 12 July 1990 the Plenary Session decided, following the interim report of the Temporary Committee on German Unification,[3] that the population of the former GDR would be represented through observer status until 1994. In this way the foundations for a change in the EP procedures were laid. In its Resolution of 12 July,[4] the EP recommended that the other institutions also invite the GDR to participate as observers. Representation of the new Community citizens in the EP should, after 1994, be resolved by a revision of the relevant legal text.

In response to the Parliament's resolution, the GDR Volkskammer named 18 members as observers in September, even though no legal norms for this had been established in the EP. From the first weekly session of September 1990 there were 18 observers present as guests – leading to speculation that this number had been stipulated by the Volkskammer, although it is not clear how it originated. In any event, the 'ceiling' of one hundred German members had not been exceeded.

After the July resolution there was a debate within the EP about the status and the legal position of the observers. During the first week of the October session, the Belgian, Dutch and especially German MEPs favoured an observer status which accorded the East Germans more or less full participatory rights, apart from the right to vote. No consensus was reached on the number of East German representatives to be admitted.

In mid-October, the president of the Bundestag, Rita Süssmuth, again named the 18 observers from the new Bundesländer. It was the outcome of the Volkskammer elections of 18 March that had determined the distribution of seats, but this was to be confirmed at the impending Bundestag elections on 2 December. The condition was laid down that the observers would have to be normally resident in the former GDR and that their mandate would come either from the Bonn Parliament or from one of the new Land governments in east Germany.

On 24 October 1990 the EP voted on the method by which the east German representatives would participate in its work. On the basis of the Galle Report to the Standing Order Committee[5] agreement was reached, largely through the combined efforts of the two biggest parliamentary groups, the Christian Democrats and the Socialists. Nonetheless the required majority of 260 votes needed to change the standing orders was by no means a foregone conclusion. The British Conservatives and the French Liberals made their consent dependent upon the waiver of the envisaged right of address.

Following a majority vote in favour (346 for, 19 against and 14 abstentions), a new article, 136a, establishing the observer status, was added to the EP's standing orders.[6] This resolution was a compromise solution:

(1) The participation of the east German observers would have no legal impact on the conduct of and the decisions taken by the EP, nor on any decisions on the number of MEPS in individual political parties.
(2) The EP could, on the recommendation of its President, invite the Bundestag to select observers who came from the former GDR and who had been democratically elected.
(3) These observers would participate in the work of the EP without having the right either to vote or to be elected.
(4) The number would be decided by the EP according to the suggestion of its President.[7]
(5) The article would apply at the very latest only until the constitutional assembly of the EP after the elections of 1994.

Despite the large majority on the actual vote, within the EP itself opinion was divided, and it is clear that a compromise solution was politically necessary.[8] After a delay of five months the Bundestag finally sent the eighteen observers from the former GDR to the EP at the end of February 1991. The distribution of seats was in accordance with the resolution of the Volkskammer in September 1990 and hence with the outcome of east Germany's elections in March of that year: the Unionspartei was allocated nine observers, the Liberals and the Alliance 90/Greens one each, the SPD five and the PDS two. The 18 observers were officially introduced into the Plenary on 10 March 1991.

Basically the observers have the same duties as an MEP, except that they are not allowed to raise their hands during voting and cannot address the Plenary. However, they are allowed to pass on their concerns to MEPs who act as a proxies. The observers are distributed among all important committees. Owing to lack of office space in Brussels and Strasbourg, they initially have to share offices either with one another or with an existing MEP. The Bundestag has to rule on the payment of daily allowances and other expenses, according to a Law on Legal Status. The EP has recommended a lump sum for expenses to pay for the upkeep of an office in the MEP's home town, so that observers can fulfil their duty to provide information to their constituents. However until now the observers have been refused the additional secretary's allowance of DM11,600, with the result that they are currently overburdened with administrative tasks.

Attempts at a solution for the post-1994 period

The issue of German representation led to the re-emergence of questions and doubts about the democratic legitimacy of the EP as a whole. Unlike the principle of equality between votes and seats observed in national elections, the distribution of seats in the member states of the EP is on a decreasing proportional basis, roughly according to eligible population. In this way the 'smaller' states are over-represented and the 'larger' ones under-represented.

Unification has led to mounting pressure for the seat distribution to become more rigorously proportional. Other member states besides Germany may now also wish to adjust their representation in a similar way. This would avoid giving the impression that Germany is using the opportunity merely for its own ends. Complete proportionality seems, however, to be out of the question. The Committee of Institutions is working on these reforms. Any changes in voting rights should also take into account the consequences of the likely enlargement of the EC.

One possibility which was strongly advocated by the Socialist Group was to confine the changes to a revision of the German mandate to include the extra 18 seats. The Christian Democrats presented two working papers: one from a French delegate, Bourlange, who was against any increase in the number of seats, and another from a German one, Bocklet, proposing a general increase in seats based on a 'regressive proportionality' which would guarantee a minimum number of seats to the smaller member states.[9] In the absence of any votes against and with three abstentions, the EP decided to demand a more truly representative seat distribution, with the aim of increasing its own legitimacy.

In the debate on 8 October 1991, the French delegates were unanimous that the new Bundesländer should be represented within the existing group of 81 German MEPs, since the principle of absolute equality of the four larger member states was laid down in the EEC Treaty and could not be prejudiced. The German delegates, on the other hand, argued for fair (proportional) representation. Even an increase of 18 seats would mean that the German people as a whole were less well represented.[10] The Socialists, supported by the Greens, felt that the demands for changes in the seat distribution were inappropriate at that time, calling instead once more for the number of German MEPs simply to be increased by eighteen from 1994. The Christian Democrats supported this initiative because their own proposals had not secured the required majority. Thus on 9 October 1991 the EP passed a common resolution,[11] demanding that the governments of the member states should suggest an increase in the number of seats for German MEPs in the IGC on political union. The German federal government accepted this resolution, thereby laying itself open to accusations (particularly from the French) of having broken its word, since it had repeatedly given assurances throughout the unification process that it would not demand any change in the balance of power within the European institutions.

In Maastricht no decision could be reached on representation; a declaration was issued (without reference to the specifically German aspects of the matter) that during 1992 a solution needed to be found to the whole question of distribution of seats in both Parliament and Commission, especially with a view to expected future accessions, by Austria, Sweden, Finland, Malta and Cyprus.[12] This solution is to apply to the next parliamentary elections. By May 1992 the Institutional Committee had reached agreement about a redistribution of MEPs. Germany would get 99 seats, and the United Kingdom, France and Italy 87 each. This would lead to a total of 567 seats in the EP.

The issue of parliamentary representation was finally resolved at the Edinburgh European Council meeting on 12 December 1992. Following the precedent set by the interim solution of allowing 18 observers from the eastern Länder, the number of seats for Germany was increased by 18. This formed part of a general increase in which, for example, the other major member states received six more seats. Although France had previously maintained that it should have equal representation with Germany, a concession on this issue was essential because the Kohl government had made agreement on more seats one of its top objectives at Edinburgh, and German support was needed for the Council's 'package' of agreements (including, for example, resolution of the Danish issue, enlargement negotiations and Community funding). The solution proposed by the British presidency was that agreement should be reached confirming the location of existing EC institutions. Strasbourg would thus remain the home of the EP, a long-held French objective. On this basis agreement on the enlargement of the EP was reached surprisingly easily.

Summary

The imminent enlargement of the EC has provoked a general debate on a redistribution of seats in all its different institutions, and on the effectiveness of these bodies. As part of this debate, it was the EP itself that took the initiative in demanding adequate representation for the population of the eastern Länder: the German government, in the interests of European integration, was careful not to make any special claims for its 16 million new citizens. The question of their representation within the Community has speeded up and intensified this debate, but did not cause it. The Maastricht declaration deliberately avoided using German unification as the driving force behind the call for redistribution.

For the present, discussion has been limited to the EP and (since Maastricht) the Commission, not the European Court of Justice or the Council. The proposed redistribution in all the member states now needs ratification in individual national parliaments, and there is a danger that some may reject it because it changes the established principle of equality in voting. It is open to question whether a new distribution will also take place in the Committee of Regions envisaged in the Maastricht Treaty.

4

MACROECONOMIC IMPLICATIONS

German unification has probably had a more immediate impact on macroeconomic policy variables than on any other area. The conditions of GEMSU had significant and long-term implications for German fiscal and monetary policy. The sudden exposure of the east German economy to competition from the west resulted in a rapid decline in output and an equally rapid rise in unemployment. The massive financial transfers from the west to integrate the former GDR into the German social market economy resulted in a large fiscal deficit. As most transfers flowed directly into consumption, rather than investment, they represented a significant stimulus to the (west) German economy and brought with them a risk of high and rising inflation, to which the Bundesbank responded by raising interest rates. This set German fiscal and monetary policies at odds with each other and created significant tensions both within Germany and in the European economy. This chapter analyses these tensions in detail.

Starting positions on EMU
Before 1989 there were, broadly speaking, two main schools of thought among supporters of EMU on how it could be achieved: those who believed that this could only happen *after* a convergence of the real economies; and those who believed that a political commitment to EMU would provide the momentum needed to achieve it. In the old FRG the Bundesbank adhered to the convergence school, as did a majority of economists and representatives of industry. But the other view, more widely shared in government circles, supported the FRG's initiation of

the whole Delors process on EMU at the Hanover European Council meeting in 1988.

In other EC member states there was more support for setting a deadline. France, in particular, wished to make rapid progress towards EMU as a means of gaining some control over the Bundesbank and thus over European monetary policy. In Britain there was no consensus on the desirability of EMU *per se*. Mrs Thatcher, following the advice of her 'special economic adviser' Professor Alan Walters, argued that the EMS and ERM were half-baked and would never work. She resisted pressure from business and City interests and kept Britain out of the ERM.[1] The compromise proposals offered by the British financial institutions for a so-called 'hard ecu' – involving a currency shadowing but not replacing the pound – broadly supported an evolutionary approach to EMU and thus had much in common with the 'convergence school' but also stopped short of endorsing the ultimate objective of a single currency.

It was against this background that the Delors Committee produced its report on EMU in April 1989.[2] This set as conditions for EMU the completion of the single market, with the four freedoms of movement of persons, goods, services and capital, as well as strengthened rules on competition and the coordinated stabilization of national economic and financial policies. The Delors Report generally favoured the Bundesbank model of an independent system of central banks and priority on price stability. At the Strasbourg European Council in December 1989, despite British objections, the EC finally decided in favour of holding an IGC on EMU, based on the recommendations of the Delors Report. But the balance between the two schools of thought on how to achieve EMU was still unresolved when the Berlin Wall was opened. This event not only resulted in a flood of east Germans to the west, it also shifted the debate within the EC away from the technicalities of EMU and towards considering the Community's response to the political revolutions taking place in central and eastern Europe.

The effect of GEMSU
During 1989–90 the accelerating pace of political developments, described in Chapter 2, meant that the option of gradually bringing about convergence before GEMSU through the progressive reform of the east German economic system was overtaken by events. In an attempt to stem the tide of migration from east to west Germany, the Cabinet Committee for German Unification, at its first meeting on 7 February 1990, decided

in principle to move rapidly to establish GEMSU.[3] The deadline of 1 July 1990 was set a couple of days after the GDR elections in March 1990. Although this decision was first and foremost politically motivated, large-scale outward migration of the best of the east German workforce would have seriously undermined the prospects of making a success of economic reform in the east.[4] The offer of GEMSU was thus intended to signal a promise of economic growth and prosperity in the east, leading to living standards on a par with those prevailing in the west.

There were a number of people who cautioned against rapid GEMSU. The Bundesbank was concerned about the implications for fiscal and monetary policy. A number of politicians, including the leader of the SPD at the time, Oskar Lafontaine, were concerned about the adjustment costs. But these views were largely swept away in the unification tide which reached full flood by March 1990, when it became clear that German unity was inevitable.

This tide also flowed through the EC debate. The French government now concerned itself with ensuring that the unified Germany would be contained, both economically and politically, within the European Community. EMU offered a means of achieving this as well as weakening the monetary hegemony of the Bundesbank by bringing it under a wider EC control. For its part the Bonn government was concerned to ensure that unification would result in a European Germany rather than a German Europe. There were therefore complementary interests in Bonn and Paris in using German unification as a catalyst for European integration. These found expression in the Kohl–Mitterrand initiative described in Chapter 2.[5] Most other member states fell into line with the Franco-German proposal, and the Dublin European Council launched two, linked, IGCs with a completion date of the end of 1991. Britain's isolated position during 1989 and 1990 prevented it from slowing down this timetable as it would have wished. The prospect of imminent German unification therefore shifted the balance between the two schools of thought on monetary union. Political objectives prevailed over the more cautious, convergence-based approach.

In what proved to be a crucial decision the Bonn government, without consulting its partners in Europe, offered the east Germans a favourable rate of exchange for old Ostmark assets. The *Staatsvertrag* of 14 June[6] extended the social market economy to the new Bundesländer. With GEMSU the non-convertible, weak Ostmark was replaced by the strong, stable Deutschmark, a move which was equivalent to a price reform. Existing claims and liabilities were exchanged at the rate of 2:1; wages and salaries and personal savings, depending upon age, up to the equivalent of DM6,000, at 1:1.

Impact on the five eastern Länder

This price reform brought about fundamental changes in the east German economy within weeks, causing massive short-term adjustment problems, despite the financial, administrative and technical assistance from west Germany. The anticipated advantages of GEMSU for east Germany – such as direct access to world financial markets and modern western technology – were more than offset by the impact of competition from both EC and world markets. The weaknesses of the east German economy – an inappropriate product mix, inefficient production methods and inadequate management skills – were exposed. The situation was made worse by the collapse of traditional eastern markets and a shift in consumer preferences towards western products.[7] This resulted in an unavoidable – and in its scale unanticipated – collapse in production and a rapid rise in the number of unemployed and short-time workers in the eastern Länder. Industrial production fell by no less than 40% in the months immediately following GEMSU (July and August) and by 50% by the fourth quarter of 1990.

By the middle of 1992 the number of those gainfully employed in eastern Germany had fallen by 3.5 million, from 10 million at the end of 1989.[8] The burden fell disproportionately on women: female unemployment increased dramatically to around 61% by spring 1992. Further evidence of this disastrous decline in the east German labour market could be seen in the large numbers of workers on 'short time', those in job creation schemes or undertaking vocational training. If these were added to the registered unemployed (1,123,202 in June 1992), the total was 2.45 million.[9] There was a further sharp rise in the number of unemployed between December 1991 and January 1992, with the expiry of many of the so-called short-time working contracts, under which wages would be paid even when no hours were actually worked. This was phased out for public service workers at the end of 1991 and for industrial workers in early 1992.

The scale and duration of the adjustment problems in eastern Germany had been seriously underestimated in the old FRG, and not only in political circles. Economic experts repeatedly revised their estimates of when the downturn in the east German economy would reach its trough, originally forecast for the spring of 1991. During 1992 the five leading

German economic research institutes predicted some recovery during that year, but only in some regions and some sectors. In the autumn of 1991 a survey revealed that hardly any east German businesses considered themselves competitive, owing to marketing difficulties, antiquated production plant, bottlenecks in investment financing, and excessive staffing levels combined with accelerating wage costs.[10]

The future development of the economy in eastern Germany will depend on attracting significant private investment and a substantial rise in productivity levels. But during 1991 there was no such substantial relocation of investment from west Germany, despite investment incentives and wage costs that were at least somewhat lower.[11] Uncertainty over property rights, the principle of restitution before compensation, poor transport infrastructure and an absence of effective public administration have all hindered the adjustment process. Moreover, a large proportion of the financial transfers to eastern Germany paid for consumption rather than capital investment.[12] For the adjustment process to be completed within ten years, the annual growth rate for the new Bundesländer would have to be around 7% higher than that in the west.[13] Estimates based on current performance in the eastern Länder suggest the adjustment process will last at least 20 years.[14] This is in stark contrast to the predictions made within political circles, where it was maintained that it would take just five years from the date of unification before the new Bundesländer became a 'thriving economic region'.

The EC Commission's assessment of the impact of GEMSU on both the east and west German Länder was more realistic than many German estimates during 1990.[15] It envisaged considerable adjustment problems and a threat to price stability in Germany, but thought that high unemployment would force down wage rates in the east more than actually happened. In reality there was considerable pressure for wage equalization, and (for those in employment) incomes of private households in the eastern Länder rose considerably after GEMSU, more or less keeping pace with rising levels of taxation and prices. Had wages matched productivity levels the pressure on east German industry would have been less intense and it might have been possible to contain the persistent double-digit inflation rates. With wage increases exceeding productivity growth, the leading German economics institutes proposed a new round of wage agreements in 1991, to bring eastern and western wages progressively in line by 1994. Although considered unrealistic at the time, such a move formed part of the broader solidarity agreement on which negotiations between unions, employers, government and opposition began in 1992.

43

The impact on Germany as a whole

A number of issues have been central to the public debate on the economic adjustment process of the eastern Länder. The most important have been the implementation, cost and efficiency of social, financial and wage policies and accompanying measures.[16] The massive costs of the reallocation resulted in German fiscal policy developing highly inflationary characteristics. There were also concerns about the impact of some policies on the German economic order (*Wirtschaftsordnung*). These issues are discussed in more detail in Chapter 5.

The main problem for German macroeconomic policy was the unprecedented mismatch between fiscal and monetary policy which developed as a result of unification. Fiscal growth was stimulated by what at times seemed like a bottomless pit of investment and above all income and other support for the east German population. On the one hand there was a political obligation to fulfil the promise of extending the social market economy to the eastern Länder. There was also inflationary pressure coming from demands for wage equalization, which was seen, at least by trade unions, as an issue of social justice and as necessary to diminish the risk of further waves of east–west migration. On this latter point there must be some doubt: a new wave of migration was more likely to be generated by a fear of unemployment in the eastern Länder.[17]

Counterbalancing these pressures to maintain an expansionary fiscal policy, the Bundesbank's determination to comply with its constitutional obligation to control inflation was unambiguous. Bundesbank views on the Deutschmark/Ostmark exchange rate had been largely overridden by the political imperative of unification. But in the weeks and months that followed GEMSU the Bundesbank made clear that its flexibility on GEMSU would not weaken its resolve on controlling inflation. In its monthly reports it repeatedly appealed to politicians, management and workers alike to exercise financial restraint. Its monetary policy was used to back up these calls, as will be seen below.

A strong or a weak Germany?

Other EC countries differed in their assessment of the potential economic policy effects of unification on the Community. Their ambivalence was illustrated by the two contradictory fears mentioned in Chapter 1. One was the fear that Germany could become a future dominant power within the Community. The Bundesbank was essentially shaping European monetary policy and west German industry stood to gain more in the long run from the opening up of its traditional eastern markets than anybody else. The British government emphasized the danger that east German firms, by being able to produce cheaper products by virtue of derogations to EC competition rules, would enjoy an unfair advantage as a 'new Hong Kong' within the Community.[18]

At the other end of the spectrum was the fear that unification would overburden the German economy and undermine its role as the 'anchor' of the EMS. As early as 1990 there was concern in other member states that the mismatch between German fiscal and monetary policy would result in higher interest rates throughout Europe. This was of particular concern in Britain which (under the Chancellorship of John Major) finally decided that 'the time was right' and joined the ERM in October 1990. Membership of the ERM meant pressure to follow the Bundesbank if it raised interest rates, which were already high in Britain. The knock-on effects of higher German interest rates came to be perceived by many in the EC as a disguised cost of unification which the Germans could shift onto their Community partners by virtue of the central role of the Bundesbank in European monetary policy.

The impact on EMU and the Maastricht negotiations

There was no clear link between the IGC on EMU, which was launched in December 1990, and GEMSU. But this did not prevent parallels being drawn. Karl Otto Pöhl, the Bundesbank president at the time, referred to GEMSU as a 'disaster', and used it to illustrate the consequences of rash moves to establish a monetary union before economic convergence had been achieved. The Bundesbank pushed the German government to insist on strict compliance with convergence criteria as a precondition for EMU. Pöhl even went as far as to argue that member states which could not meet the criteria should be allowed to follow at a slower pace. There would therefore be a two-tier currency union, with only a few of the member states in the first tier.[19] Pöhl's important statement was seen at the time as a stab in the back for Chancellor Kohl, who had publicly fixed the timing of GEMSU without prior arrangement with the Bundesbank and was pressing for EMU. In other words, while unification contributed to an acceleration of the EMU process and to the addition of the European political union objectives, its impact did not continue much beyond the summer of 1990 and the German negotiating position was focused once more on convergence criteria.

The Maastricht Treaty

The agreement on EMU constituted the core of the Maastricht agreement on a Treaty on European Union. The objectives were the irrevocable fixing of European exchange rates as a prelude to the introduction of a common currency as well as a commitment to the realization of a common monetary and exchange-rate policy. A European Monetary Institute was to be established in the second stage of EMU and to be directed and managed by a Council. By 31 December 1996 at the latest, an assembly of the Heads of State or Government, acting by qualified majority, was to decide whether a majority of the member states fulfilled the necessary conditions for the adoption of a single currency and if and when the third stage of EMU should be implemented. These conditions covered the annual fiscal deficit (not more than 3% of GDP), the size of the total public debt (not more than 60% of GDP) and the rate of inflation (an average rate of within 1.5% of the average of the three 'best' rates of inflation in the EC). If this decision had not been reached by 1997, then the final stage of EMU would automatically take effect from 1 January 1999 for each country in a position to fulfil the convergence criteria as approved by Heads of State or Government. This also opened up the possibility of a 'mini-EMU' from 1999 with a minority of member states, which could then introduce the ecu as a common currency in their own countries.

The Maastricht agreement was broadly in line with the views of the major political parties in the Bundestag.[20] The federal government and the Bundesbank apparently cooperated well enough during the negotiations, and were successful in achieving their main objectives: priority for price stability, independence for the central bank, and no financing of national budget deficits. Provisions were also included on ways of scrutinizing national deficits and, in the event of inaction by the national government, initiating sanctions proceedings should reference values be continuously exceeded.[21]

In Maastricht, however, Chancellor Kohl gave up his own and the Bundesbank's hopes of any principle of linkage between EMU and the realization of a political union. The absence of a strong commitment to political union was therefore criticized by many in Germany, including the Bundesbank, which has no remit for European political union.[22] Britain, seeing monetary union as a market-orientated process rather than a political act of union, sought to avoid specific commitments. But London failed in its attempt to 'sell' its 'hard ecu' proposals to its Community partners.[23] Prime Minister Major did nonetheless secure from the negotiations the 'Protocol on certain provisions relating to the

United Kingdom'. This opt-out released Britain from any commitment to enter the third stage of EMU, which in any case could only be made after consultation with the British Parliament. The European Council would then make its assessment based on convergence criteria. Until such time Britain is excluded from certain provisions relating to convergence and the necessary procedures for their implementation, for example the independence of the national central bank. Major described the outcome of Maastricht as 'game, set and match for Britain'.[24] But as subsequent events showed, this was not enough to ensure the smooth passage of the Treaty through the House of Commons.

The economic impact of unification on Germany's neighbours

In the second half of 1990 growth in all major industrial nations began to decelerate and the British economy had all the hallmarks of a recession. German unification at first injected new life into the European economy, thanks to an added 2.3% growth in German GNP. The EC Commission estimated there was a 0.5% rise in Community GNP in 1990/91 as the result of increased demand in eastern Germany. As German companies did not have the capacity to supply all this demand, Germany's substantial surplus in external trade actually swung into a deficit in 1991. All this should have been to the benefit of Germany's competitors. But the locomotive effect was short-lived.[25] By 1992 growth in Germany was no longer compensating for the deflationary effects of high interest rates, and towards the end of the year the German economy also began to move into recession.[26]

The swing in Germany's balance of payments could well have led to a potential tightening of the already scarce availability of international capital and thus a potential loss to the poorer members of the EC. But economists in the EC Commission and elsewhere have tended to downplay this effect.[27] First, taken as a whole, financial transfers to east Germany have not overburdened the flexible international capital markets. Second, the channelling of international investment activity into the new Bundesländer has been moderate and should not disadvantage the poorer regions of the Community, which benefited from the increase in German imports throughout 1991. It is nonetheless evident that high German interest rates have attracted foreign capital into the country and will continue to do so.[28] The capital funds of foreign investors have been rising continuously since the second half of 1990 and have become an important contribution towards covering the cost of the large rise in public-sector borrowing.

In addition to the massive transfers to the east, the German public purse also had to cover undertakings for financial assistance to the former Soviet Union (paying for the rehousing of troops) and its legal successors (some DM3.25bn), together with its share of the costs of the Gulf war (DM11.5bn).[29] As if this were not enough, there is the burden of financing the Treuhandanstalt, the additional costs of moving the capital to Berlin and DM300bn in former GDR debt. Germany will therefore remain saddled with a large public debt for some time as efforts to make substantial reductions in spending have not yet had results (see Chapter 5). The government's efforts have been severely criticized by the economic research institutes.[30]

The inflationary effect of German unification has been far less severe than was feared. The highest interim value for 1991 was 4.4% in July – higher than Germany's psychologically acceptable barrier of 4%, but nonetheless below the ERM average.[31] The Bundesbank's target in 1991–2 was to cut inflation to 2% in the medium term.[32] While its tight monetary policy had some success in containing German inflation and thus ensuring that the Deutschmark maintained its role as the stable 'anchor' currency in the ERM, it was not without costs for other countries in terms of higher interest rates.

In February 1991 the Bundesbank raised both the discount and the internationally important Lombard rate, to 6.5% and 9% respectively. In August they were raised again, to 7% and 9.25% respectively (see Figure 4.1). Central banks in several EC countries were reluctantly forced to follow suit, owing to the fixed exchange-rate regime of the EMS, although for a time countries with falling growth rates or even recessionary tendencies, such as Britain and Spain, actually reduced interest rates instead in an attempt to revive their flagging economies. This was possible in Britain because interest rates had been so high between 1989 and 1991.

Both Bonn and Frankfurt considered the Bundesbank's actions to be proof of its independence. Given its mandate to ensure price stability, interest rate rises were unavoidable. A number of other EC countries, including Britain, criticized the Bundesbank's *Alleingang* during a period in the Community's history which should have been one of close cooperation in economic and monetary matters.[33] This criticism, fuelled by fears of damage to the European and world economy, became all the more pronounced following the third hike in German interest rates in December 1991.[34] At this point France accused the Bundesbank of pursuing policies that were 'a contradiction of the spirit of Maastricht'.[35]

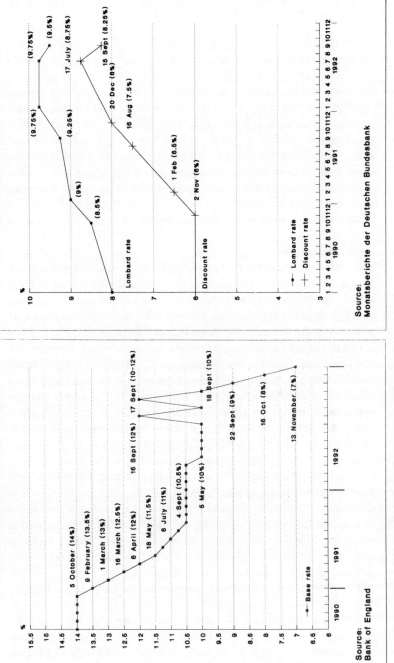

Figure 4.1 Interest rate changes in Britain and Germany

(a) Interest rate changes in Britain

5 October (14%)
9 February (13.5%)
1 March (13%)
16 March (12.5%)
6 April (12%)
18 May (11.5%)
8 July (11%)
4 Sept (10.5%)
5 May (10%)
16 Sept (12%)
17 Sept (10-12%)
18 Sept (10%)
22 Sept (9%)
16 Oct (8%)
13 November (7%)

← Base rate

Source:
Bank of England

(b) Interest rate changes in Germany

(9.75%)
(9.75%)
(9.5%)
(9.25%)
(9%)
(9.25%)
(8.5%)
17 July (8.75%)
15 Sept (8.25%)
20 Dec (8%)
16 Aug (7.5%)
1 Feb (6.5%)
2 Nov (6%)

Lombard rate
Discount rate

Lombard rate
Discount rate

Source:
Monatsberichte der Deutschen Bundesbank

For its part, however, the Bundesbank was determined to give an unmistakable signal to German trade unions and employers of the need for wage restraint.

Things became critical in the summer of 1992 when the Bundesbank raised its discount rate from 8% to 8.75% on the grounds that the growth in German money supply was still above target (9% in contrast to the anticipated 3.5–5.5%).[36] Conscious of the wider implications of such rises, the Bundesbank did not increase the Lombard rate. But clearly, German unification and its consequential impact on prices and interest rates limited room for manoeuvre in British interest rate policy and that of several southern EC member states; in this sense some of the costs of unification were borne by Germany's neighbours.

Impact on Britain

The impact was nowhere more directly perceived than in Britain, where high interest rates were particularly painful because of the high levels of private indebtedness. During the boom of the 1980s many people had bought houses at inflated prices. Recession and high interest rates meant a decline in the value of property and high debt repayments. This had a depressive effect on the housing market and the economy as a whole, and, combined with the underlying weakness of the British economy, raised doubts about the viability of Britain remaining in the ERM if it meant sustaining high rates of interest – a point which was seized upon by opponents of Britain's participation in the ERM and those who sought to block ratification of the Maastricht Treaty in the House of Commons. The credibility of Britain's position in the ERM depended, in part, on the credibility of the commitment, made by the EC in Maastricht, to move towards EMU. After the 'no' vote in the Danish referendum in June 1992, doubts began to emerge about the proposed timetable, and weak currencies came under increased market pressure. Speculation mounted that sterling would ultimately be forced to devalue, and despite assurances to the contrary from the British government, sterling was pulled out of the ERM on 16 September 1992 (known as 'Black Wednesday'). This was a very serious blow to the credibility of the British government's economic and European policies and encouraged the Eurosceptics in both the Conservative party and the country as a whole.

It is difficult to measure the extent to which German unification influenced the exit of Britain from the ERM and the associated rise in opposition to the Maastricht agreement. Arguably Britain had joined the ERM at the 'wrong' rate (DM2.85 to the pound) and at the wrong time (just after German unification, when the pressure on German interest rates was at its height and the European and world economies were entering a recession). It had been an open secret that the Bundesbank felt the rate was wrong and was unhappy about Britain's unilateral decision on the terms of sterling's entry. The government had also attempted, ultimately in vain, to link sterling to the stable Deutschmark and thus to the German economy through the ERM, despite the underlying weakness of the British economy. In other words there was still a great deal to do by way of convergence. Moreover, there were serious tensions within the EMS as a result of the divergences between US and German interest rates: in an attempt to revive the American economy, the US Federal Reserve had reduced rates to 3%.

Nevertheless, there was still a perception in Britain during 1992 that the country's economic problems were the result of the Bundesbank's attempts to contain the inflation created by unification. It was hardly surprising that the Chancellor of the Exchequer, Norman Lamont, chose the Bundesbank as the scapegoat for the collapse of Britain's economic strategy on the grounds that it had failed to help and had even fed speculation on the pound. What was more remarkable was the fact that the average house-buyer was conscious of the direct financial impact of decisions taken in Frankfurt.[37]

Conclusions

German unification had a short-term effect on the balance between those favouring rapid integration and moves towards monetary union and those favouring a more cautious approach, but almost as soon as GEMSU had taken place and a deadline had been set for the completion of the IGC on EMU, the cautious approach returned to the fore, and with it the determination of the Bundesbank to regain control in its fight against inflation. The difficulties that hit the EC during 1992 raised doubts about the viability of the EMU objective, given that the ERM had failed to withstand the test of that year. Alignments are, of course, possible during the first stage of EMU, but the project's credibility was damaged. In Britain the fact that sterling was forced out of the ERM had the effect of undermining the government's credibility and thus its ability to steer the ratification of Maastricht through the Commons in the face of opposition from its own 'Eurosceptic' rebels. German unification therefore had a real effect on both the European economy and the European integration process.

5

THE IMPACT ON THE GERMAN AND EC REGULATORY FRAMEWORKS

The relative success of the German attempt to combine economic growth with social cohesion became a model for others within the Community. But how well has the German economy withstood the pressures of absorbing the GDR? Has unification tended to create an *économie dominante* or to weaken German industry? Is Germany emerging from the process of unification with its reputation as a model federal, social market economy enhanced or its cohesion undermined? This chapter seeks to address these questions by considering how two of the main elements of the 'German model' are affected: first, the role of the state as a regulator of the market – a central issue here is the balance between competition on the one hand and preserving jobs and investment in the five new Länder on the other; and, second, the reallocation mechanisms which are an important factor in the social market economy.

Any change in Germany will have implications for the Community. If the balance favours competition and liberal structures in the five new Länder, this would ensure a regime compatible with the objectives of a liberal internal market. It might even bring about changes in sectors in the old Länder where vested interests have hitherto opposed EC-wide liberalization. If, on the other hand, the balance favours more closed structures as the price for promoting investment and jobs in the east, this works against general EC liberalization. If Germany is obliged to continue to adopt a more interventionist approach than was the accepted norm in the old FRG, this may also have implications for the debate on EC industrial policy, which is finely balanced between those seeking more active policies and those in favour of more *laissez-faire* approaches. Finally, the already high costs of unification could well make Germany reluctant to provide more resources for structural funds or other forms of reallocation within the Community.

The legal aspects of regulatory policy have been largely resolved. The *Staatsvertrag* and *Einigungsvertrag*, as noted in Chapter 2, effectively extended the old west German laws to include the five eastern Länder, with a few time-limited exemptions. This chapter considers how these policies are actually applied in the very different circumstances of east Germany and how this impinges on the established German and EC policy approaches. It draws on a number of case-studies, which are illustrated in more detail in Chapters 6–9. It is clear that markets as well as policies are influencing and being influenced by unification, and that structures established before either west German or EC disciplines on competition applied will influence the German market, and thus the European market, for many years to come.

With regard to the reallocation functions of the state, such as in the provision of subsidies to maintain production, social security benefits or job creation schemes, there is a more direct relationship between policy and practice: expenditure on social programmes and job retention policies accounts for most of the net financial transfers of public funds from west to east Germany – a total of DM160bn in 1992, and a similar sum is envisaged for 1993.

The challenge
Unification, as has been stated many times, has posed a uniquely difficult task for Germany and, for that matter, the Community. The objective – to bring about systemic change from a centrally planned economy to a (social) market economy – had to be achieved without alienating political support for the process in both east and west Germany. Privatization and decentralization were the key tasks in the east German economy.

The highly centralized industrial structure of the GDR was characterized by vertically and horizontally organized *Kombinate*. These generally brought together the enterprises in any given sector and were under the control of either national sponsoring ministries or regional bodies, depending upon their importance for the economy. Breaking up the *Kombinate* in order to ensure both a competitive market structure and more efficient production was a massive task. It was also necessary to recreate a *Mittelstand* (small and medium-sized companies up to 500 employees) more or less from scratch if there was to be decentralization of industrial power and any approximation to the successful west German structure. Table 5.1 shows how some 80% of east German manufacturing industry was controlled by companies of over 1,000 employees, compared with about 40% in the west. It clearly shows the weakness of the *Mittelstand* in the east, where it was only to be found in the craft and service sectors, unlike in west Germany, where it has been the mainstay of economic success.

Table 5.1 Manufacturing industry: size of company

No. of employees	Percentage of industry	
	GDR	FRG
1–50	0.2	8.7
51–500	9.4	38.1
501–1000	10.8	13.3
Over 1000	79.8	39.9

Source: Statistisches Bundesamt and Institut für Angewandte Wirtschaftsforschung, 1990.

The task of reforming and restructuring the east German economy, and industry in particular, was made very much harder by the early move to establish GEMSU on 1 July 1990. Whatever the political reasons, the impact of opening the east to competition from the west meant that much of east German industry became uncompetitive virtually overnight. The actual or impending collapse of east German industry obviously influenced policy decisions after July 1990.

The main task of privatizing the east German economy fell to the Treuhandanstalt (THA), the trust fund administration which was set up on 1 March 1990 under Hans Modrow's government. Its role will be examined in greater detail below, and in the case-studies. There were other important actors in the period immediately following the opening of the Berlin Wall, and to a greater or lesser extent until formal unification. Private sector companies, predominantly from west Germany but also from other countries, were and remain key players in decisions affecting the east German economy. The east German government took important decisions affecting the process of restructuring and privatization. During the course of 1990 west German authorities at all levels, but in particular the Federal Ministry of Economics, became more and more involved in decisions affecting the structure of east German industry. The competition authorities in both parts of Germany also played important roles.

Key decision–makers

The private sector response
A good number of west German firms already had long-established links with the east German *Kombinate* in their sectors. After November 1989 they began to intensify these links, and firms not already engaged began to take an active interest in the east German market. Given the uncertainty surrounding the course of political and economic reform in the GDR, the initial response of most western firms was to seek cooperation agreements with their eastern partners. Some companies were prepared to commit themselves to investment in the east. Both Volkswagen and Siemens announced that they would sign joint ventures with *Kombinate* as soon as it became clear what the legal basis for investment would be. Such projects began to be implemented when the GDR government allowed wholly foreign-owned subsidiaries from early March 1990 (originally only a 49% holding by foreign firms had been possible). These decisions constituted political statements in support of unification rather than decisions based purely on economic considerations. In many cases the firms concerned were investing in what had once been their own plants or even company headquarters.

Western – primarily west German – interest focused on those sectors in which barriers to market access were likely to remain after unification: sectors in which factors such as distribution networks, natural monopolies, proximity to the customer or very high transport costs demanded a local presence to ensure effective supply. Thus the initial interest was in financial services (where branch networks are an important prerequisite of access), in energy (where there are local natural monopolies) and in cement (because of high transport costs). In all cases negotiations began early in 1990 and, with some notable exceptions, were not completed until after GEMSU. Thus in the eleven months between the opening of the Berlin Wall and political unification, agreements or acquisitions were concluded that have already determined the structure of important parts of the east German economy.

In the *electricity sector* (see Chapter 7) west German power companies, such as RWE, had been cooperating with the industry in the east for many years. RWE has the greatest experience of generating power from lignite in a relatively clean and efficient fashion. Other firms, such as PreußenElektra, had also signed cooperation agreements with the eastern power generators. In the early months of 1990 cooperation intensified and agreements were made to assist in the modernization of eastern power generation and distribution networks and to reduce environmental pollution. In March 1990 RWE, Bayernwerk and PreußenElektra reached agreements with the eastern power *Kombinate* to this effect.[1] At the same time there was an understanding between the eastern generators and distributors that massive western investment was needed if the security of supply was to be guaranteed.

In the *shipbuilding sector* (see Chapter 9) there were early meetings between the industry in the east and that in the west. These led to an agreement that west German shipyards would provide advice on improving productivity and that the VSM Verband, the west German sectoral association, would also represent east German shipbuilding interests in the EC and OECD negotiations. One of the major problems in shipbuilding is the persistent surplus capacity, and both the EC and OECD have regimes in place which seek to limit national subsidies. One of the initial issues for the western shipyards was to avoid additional east German capacity upsetting this delicate political balance.

There were similar contacts and a similar process of assessment in the *steel industry*. The east German industry soon proved to be largely obsolete.[2] Even the more productive plants, such as the oxygen steel plant in Eisenhüttenstadt, would have needed considerable investment in order to meet the necessary standards to compete internationally. Such large-scale investment would, on the other hand, have risked exacerbating surplus capacity. A study by the Rheinlandwestfälisches Wirtschaftsinstitut suggested that one half of the GDR's 8-million-tonne steel capacity would have to be cut. Clearly, as long as west German producers were faced with surplus capacity in the European steel industry generally, there was no incentive to maintain capacity in the eastern Länder. They preferred instead to help ensure higher capacity utilization of west German plants, to improve their own market position vis-à-vis their European and international competitors.

Although it was clear by this time that unification was to occur, there were still important uncertainties for investors, particularly in manufacturing, where products could generally be supplied from western plants. Having assessed the state of some of the eastern capital equipment, western firms were reluctant to invest until they knew the conditions under which such plants were to operate. For example, it was not clear whether there would be a transitional period in which there would not be parity between the Deutschmark and the Ostmark.

The GDR authorities

In the early months of 1990 the GDR government was the main negotiating partner for western firms. In the insurance sector, for example, the Council of Ministers (*Ministerrat*) of the GDR decided on 3 March to end the state monopoly and create the Deutsche Versicherungs AG. At the same time it was agreed that, from 1 May 1990, the west German firm Allianz would take the maximum allowed 49% share in Deutsche Versicherung, the other 51% to be held by the Treuhand. The east German government had considered a variety of options, including splitting the insurance sector into a number of regional companies. This would have enabled a range of companies to acquire a presence in the east German sector, but it was rejected on the grounds that the deal with Allianz offered both prudential security for the sector and the retention of jobs. In practice, however, officials in the east German government made no real effort to talk to other companies. As the case-study in Chapter 6 shows, opposition to the deal from both the east German Volkskammer and the west German and EC competition authorities later forced some modest liberalization, but the essential structure of the deal struck between the Modrow government and Allianz remained.

The case of *banking* also illustrates the role of the east German authorities. In early March 1990 the Modrow government reformed the banking system by turning the old Staatsbank into an independent central bank and a commercial banking operation, the Deutsche Kreditbank. This commercial operation soon decided that it had neither the capital nor the know-how to compete with the major western banks. Contacts were therefore immediately made with the west German banks and in particular the Deutsche Bank to discuss cooperation. The arrangement was tailored to ensure that it did not eliminate all competition and thus avoided the sort of criticism provoked by the Allianz deal. The Deutsche Bank therefore bid for only 100 of the 170 branches of the Deutsche Kreditbank. But once again the essence of the deal was struck at a time when the only body with authority to influence it was the east German government.

The structure of the *energy sector* was similarly determined by an agreement between the responsible GDR officials and the three major west German power companies in early 1990, when the latter sought regulatory changes that would enable them to acquire the whole chain.[3] East German officials were willing to comply because access to financial resources from the west to ensure security of supply and to reduce environmental pollution was more important than competition. As the case-study in Chapter 7 shows, modifications were made, as they were in insurance, but again the deal struck in January or February determined the structure of the sector.

The Federal Cartel Office

Although the west German competition policies did not apply until unification, the Federal Cartel Office in West Berlin had a role in the sense that it is legally empowered to investigate actions outside the FRG which impinge upon competition in the west German market. It also argued during the summer of 1990 that as west German law and EC competition law would apply to the territory of the GDR after unification, the east German ministries should operate 'as if' they already applied. The Cartel Office was aware of the danger of anti-competitive developments in the GDR from an early stage; in March 1990 its President argued that 'we must ensure that east German state monopolies are not simply transformed into private monopolies'.[4]

The Cartel Office's basic policy stance was that mergers and other concentrations did not threaten competition provided they did not exclude new entrants from the east German market. In most cases the opening of the inner-German border provided significant opportunities for new entrants and thus an increase in competition, so that there was little need for detailed investigation. The Cartel Office did, however, look closely at the cases in which the whole industry was being acquired and which could thus preclude new market entrants, such as in energy, insurance and banking. Its rulings are described in the case-studies in the following chapters.

The Aufsichtsamt für Wettbewerbsschutz

Given the limited competence of the west German competition authorities, the burden of championing competition during the period before unification fell onto the brand-new east German competition authority, the *Aufsichtsamt für Wettbewerbsschutz* (AfW). The AfW was set up in April 1990, at a time when the furore over the Allianz acquisition was at its peak, although it had no legal force until the end of June. Its director defined its objective during what was a very active phase of major mergers as 'do[ing] everything possible to prevent the new shoots of the market economy being trampled under foot'.[5]

The AfW faced an uphill struggle from the beginning. First of all, many of the important concentration agreements were already being considered when it was created. It also had a fairly modest staff of some

50 people, although its proximity to the west German Cartel Office (both were in Berlin) meant that the two could and did cooperate. The resources of the AfW were also thinly spread. In addition to concentrations, it had to investigate potential unfair pricing practices, a particularly sensitive area at a time of generally rising prices. The law establishing the AfW made no clear separation between consideration of the competition and the political or industrial aspects of any concentration, and the AfW came under the control of the east German Ministry of Economics. In the west, by contrast, the Cartel Office is responsible for assessing takeover bids purely on the basis of competition criteria. The law allows for some flexibility: the so-called *Ministererlaß* means that the responsible economics minister can overrule the Cartel Office and allow a concentration to go ahead even if it does inhibit competition, but it must do so openly.

On 3 July 1990 the AfW approved the Allianz and Deutsche Bank acquisitions on similar grounds to those given by the Federal Cartel Office, but rejected the agreement on the power industry, arguing that 'it could never approve this and that it was up to the Ministry of Economics to give its consent if it wished the deal to go ahead' for reasons of broader public interest. The AfW therefore tried its best to become a champion of competition on the model of the western Cartel Office, but, given the time and resources available to it, its impact was always going to be limited. On unification the resources of the AfW and about half of its personnel were taken over by the Cartel Office.

The European Commission
The third competition authority with an interest in developments in the GDR was the European Commission, or to be more precise Directorate General IV (DGIV). In mid-May 1990, Sir Leon Brittan, Commissioner with responsibility for competition, was beginning to express concern about a number of the major agreements concluded between west and east German companies, over which the EC had no jurisdiction.[6] In legal terms the Commission's position was analogous to that of the Cartel Office, only weaker. Under Articles 85 and 86 (EEC) the Commission claimed powers to act against concentrations outside the EC which had an effect on competition within the EC. In reality such an effects doctrine was unusable. At best it was controversial, at least among non-EC countries. In the highly charged conditions of German unification, when the maintenance of a viable financial system or power network was at stake, it is difficult to see how the Commission really could have intervened. It probably used reference to its ultimate legal powers in an

attempt to gain some influence over decision-makers in Bonn and East Berlin. In July 1990 Sir Leon Brittan wrote to both east and west German ministers of economics urging them, and in particular the east German minister Pohl, to act 'as if' the EC treaty provisions already applied.[7]

Impact of the competition authorities

None of the competition authorities had a really decisive influence on whether or not deals went ahead during the months before unification, though they did exert a moderating influence. The officials in the east German ministries were not experienced in dealing with competition policy. They were much more skilled as planners and thus favoured the certainty of having west German Deutschmarks over any risky experimentation with competitive markets. There was also a genuine concern about jobs and the integrity of the markets concerned, such as the need to ensure the security of power supplies. In retrospect these fears were exaggerated, and were clearly played on by western firms, but few people at the time realized that east German industry would decline so dramatically, thus reducing energy consumption and averting the danger of a supply shortage. What is clear is that in important instances powerful west German companies were able to dictate to east German regulatory agencies. This is not surprising given the relative balance of influence. West German firms offered large-scale capital resources and were therefore in a strong negotiating position.

There were some fairly lonely voices, such as from the west German *Monopolkommission*, arguing that unification should be used as a means of injecting more competition into the west German system, rather than simply extending that system and its market structures to the whole of Germany.[8] Given that the unification process was unsettling for both German industry and regulators alike, it was not surprising that any experimentation gained little support.

The Treuhandanstalt

The Treuhand's privatization mission

The Treuhandanstalt was created exclusively for dealing with the privatization of some 8,000 east German *Kombinate* and *Volkseigene Betriebe* (collectives). It was given a decisive role in the process of transforming east Germany into a market economy. Established on 1 March 1990 by the Modrow government with a central office and 15 regional offices, it was not given full legal powers until 17 June 1990, in the *Treuhandgesetz*, when it took over all state property and nationalized industries. These powers were confirmed in Article 25 of the *Einigungsvertrag*. After unification the Treuhand came under the direction of a board of governors appointed by the federal government, and became accountable to the Federal Minister of Finance.

According to the Treuhand law the tasks of the THA are as follows:

(1) privatization and administration of productive all-state holdings;
(2) adaptation to the needs of the market economy by privatizing as many companies as possible while ensuring their competitiveness and maintaining existing and creating new employment opportunities;
(3) 'unbundling' of existing combines and the creation of companies able to survive under market conditions;
(4) provision of land for economic development; and
(5) privatization and reorganization of public holdings of agricultural combines.

In order to help the THA to satisfy itself that these conditions are met, a corporate plan is required from any company acquiring a THA company, along with a two-year guarantee that it will not dispose of land acquired. This is to prevent property speculators acquiring companies merely in order to obtain land. The corporate plan must include undertakings on the number of jobs that will be retained for a two-year period, as well as information on planned investment and how this will be financed. Such undertakings go beyond normal practice, even for the privatization of public assets, and limit the freedom of action of the management. Such limitations came as something of a surprise for foreign companies, especially British, American and Japanese firms, accustomed as they are to having a free hand to dispose of any assets they control. This suggests that the THA approach to privatization differs from that taken by certain OECD countries, or for that matter some developing countries during the 1980s. This was only to be expected, given that an entire economy was being privatized in the shortest possible time, but it remains an open question as to whether the THA conditions have had a material effect in reducing the number of foreign investors in east Germany.

On balance the THA has made good progress towards achieving its objectives, despite a small number of irregularities in its operations, especially before unification.[9] In order to achieve its privatization objectives it has, however, been obliged to exempt purchasers from any obligation to correct existing ecological damage, and in order to induce or encourage investors to guarantee employment it has also had to offer reductions in the purchase price.

The original total of 8,000 companies had in fact grown to over 11,500 in two years, through the results of splitting existing *Kombinate*. Of the 6,409 companies still on the books of the THA, over 1,000 are scheduled for liquidation, leaving just over 5,000 still to be sold. Table 5.2 shows that foreign participation in the privatization process has been substantial.

Table 5.2 Foreign investors, 31 May 1992

Country	Investment (million DM)	Employment promised	Privatizations
Austria	503	9,015	48
Belgium	87	2,804	9
Denmark	372	2,524	16
France	2,703	18,350	51
Great Britain	1,626	14,387	68
Italy	377	2,920	15
Netherlands	912	5,854	33
Sweden	89	3,351	19
Switzerland	682	14,148	69
USA	1,581	6,168	27
Others	2,623	27,105	35
Total	11,555	106,626	390

Source: *Monatsinformation der THA*, 31 May 1992.

The restructuring activities of the Treuhand

Although there was always a certain industrial restructuring function involved in privatization, the political pressure for the THA to play a more active role increased from the spring of 1991 for a number of reasons.

First, there was concern about the rapid decline in employment in east Germany. This led to increased pressure on the THA to place more emphasis on restructuring uncompetitive companies and bringing them back to health rather than liquidating them. For some time the THA resisted such pressure from trade unions and politicians for fear that it would be distracted from its primary task of privatization. However, by early 1991 it became clear that the company closures were running at a rate that was creating considerable political opposition in the new Länder and threatening to provoke active opposition to rationalization measures from trade unions. This could have jeopardized privatization, which rarely occurred without any loss of jobs. On 17 July 1991 the THA concluded an agreement with trade unions, employers and the new Länder governments to establish short-term employment creation undertakings (*Gesellschaften zur Arbeitsförderung, Beschäftigung und Strukturentwicklung*, or ABSs). East German employees laid off as part of a rationalization programme or plant closure are taken on the ABSs and offered retraining or places on job creation programmes, which are managed by the THA and funded by the west German Federal Office for Labour as part of the social programme for the east.[10]

The ABSs were opposed by industry in the west. The Confederation of German Industry (*Bundesverband der Deutschen Industrie*, BDI) saw them as conflicting with the *Ordnungspolitik*. The BDI feared that because the ABSs were subsidized by the Office of Labour they would be able to offer low prices and thus mop up most of the smaller public works contracts, thereby crowding out desired investment by small and medium-sized companies in the east, militating against the objective of creating an effective *Mittelstand* there. Perversely the ABSs could therefore undermine the long-term prospects for stable employment growth, with the result that there would be pressure to keep them in existence. In other words there was a risk that they would become a permanent feature of the economy. The financial costs of such measures were also an important consideration.

There was a second, related concern about the demise of east German, i.e. locally controlled, industry or at least companies that were identified with the local communities in the east. This was most clearly articulated by a group of CDU members of the Bundestag from the new Länder,[11] which has argued that east Germany is in danger of losing all indigenous industry, as firms are either acquired by west German or foreign firms or go bankrupt under the pressure of competition. The remedy proposed is for the THA to operate as a state holding company, similar to those owning public enterprise in other EC member states. This would entail owning and investing in important east German industries in order to turn them into profitable companies able to compete on international markets; they would then be privatized by floating shares on the stock exchanges. The policy would be a temporary measure and all companies would ultimately be sold. But the proposers argue that it would reverse the current trend towards a de-industrialization of east Germany.

The issue here, of course, is whether there is a case for having industries which are identified as being 'east' German, and seems to reflect a residual desire to retain some form of east German identity. The Ministry of Finance, which controls the THA, does not favour moving down a path that could result in Germany creating a large state holding company. Such an explicit industrial policy would certainly be at odds with the established non-interventionist *Ordnungspolitik*. Indeed the Bonn government has consistently complained about unfair competition from such companies in other EC member states, particularly in Italy. In principle there is no reason why the German concept of *Ordnungspolitik* should not be as flexible with regard to industrial policy as it has been with regard to competition policy (when the FRG authorities chose investment in preference to competition). In reality, however, it is much less likely that such a visible form of intervention would be politically acceptable, particularly to other members states which have been tolerant of the Treuhand's activities in the short run because of the exceptional circumstances, but which would object if such intervention were maintained on a long-run basis.

Proposals have also been put forward to make support from the Treuhand more automatic, such as the introduction of a degressive temporary employment subsidy of up to 50% of wage costs and the provision of automatic matching investment grants for capital investment undertaken in east Germany. The support schemes would be phased out after a number of years.[12] The federal government has not yet responded to these proposals. Regardless of whether or not they result in any changes of policy, they do show that there is pressure for more active measures to promote industrial activity in the five new Länder.

The European Commission's handling of the Treuhand

There can be little doubt that even some of the current actions of the Treuhand already fall into the category of state support for industry. The European Commission, and in particular the competition authorities in DGIV, therefore have a duty to ensure that these national subsidies are consistent with the treaty provisions. The Treaty of Rome allows exceptions to the general ban on all state subsidies, on condition that the European Commission must be notified of aid programmes and approve exemptions.

In September 1991 the Commission came to a general understanding on how to handle the THA's operations, observing that the activities of the THA did indeed constitute a subsidy and therefore needed to be notified. The Commission made clear that in assessing each notification it would bear in mind the scale and exceptional nature of the task facing the THA. In order to simplify matters and to reduce the number of cases that had to be notified and assessed, the Commission laid down a number of guidelines. It decided that it would not consider as subsidies the assumption by the THA of old debts or the costs of environmental cleansing measures resulting from pollution while the company concerned was under east German control. The provision of credit to maintain the liquidity of companies or export credits provided by the THA would, on the other hand, be seen as subsidies but would be approved on the condition that they were notified to the Commission. In this way the Commission hopes to be able to pursue a relatively flexible policy while at the same time ensuring that THA aid is transparent.

On privatization, the Commission decided that transactions would be assumed not to involve any subsidization if the asset is offered through an open tender, i.e. that the sale is open to all comers, and sold to the highest bidder. However, the THA does not always sell to the highest bidder in monetary terms, since part of its remit is to preserve as many jobs as possible, and it is thus prepared to consider a lower sale price if a company offers to guarantee more jobs. All such cases that are agreed by the central Treuhand office in Berlin have to be notified to the Commission for its approval.

Finally, the Commission pays special attention to the credits or credit guarantees provided by the THA to maintain production in companies it still holds. The EC precedent, established over many years, is that production subsidies are generally not acceptable, whereas subsidies to assist with adjustment or redeployment of labour are. In this context the Commission would have to assess any move to make the THA into a form of state holding company. The question of how to handle state holding companies, or public enterprise in general, is a controversial item of discussion in the EC. A number of governments are decidedly unhappy about recent Commission forays into the area of public enterprise, and there might be pressure from other member states for the THA to be treated in the same fashion.

On balance, the Commission's policy is flexible (at least for the time being), provided that the THA maintains transparency in its support. The Commission fully recognizes the task the THA and German government face and does not wish to make this any harder, but it has made clear that it will not tolerate indefinite subsidies. At present neither the Commission nor the German authorities are making any estimate about how long the THA will have to support some of its holdings.

Reallocation mechanisms

Testing the German social consensus

The old FRG was characterized by a relatively high degree of social consensus. At a national level this was based on the concept of the social market economy, in which the state provides a safety net for those who are, *inter alia*, affected by economic structural change. Germany's federal structure also requires a reallocation of funds among the Länder by means of the so-called *Finanzausgleich*. Thus the interstate transfers and the payments for social security or unemployment benefit together provide for the major part of the reallocation of resources in the old FRG.

Unification and the effort of extending the social support system to the population of the new Länder, as well as paying for the restructuring if not the reconstruction of the east German economy, are putting a tremendous strain on the social consensus that facilitates reallocation, and are threatening the social component of the social market economy. The claims by the east German population to the same level of social provision as is provided in the west – effectively promised to them with German unification – have required significant levels of public intervention. The scale of social transfer payments has exceeded levels that have come to be acceptable within the old FRG.

Article 7 of the *Einigungsvertrag* extended the existing FRG *Finanzausgleich* system to the new Länder. But it did so with a number of exceptions, concerning the distribution of tax revenues, the base for local taxes in the Länder (*Gemeinschaftssteuer*) and the redistribution of revenue among the Länder. For various reasons, the new Länder will not be brought fully into the system of financial redistribution until 1994. For example, the system in the old FRG assumes that the financial needs of the population are the same regardless of where they live, and thus financial calculations for any one Land are based purely on population. As the needs of the population in the new Länder are currently higher than those of citizens in the old Länder, given the former's lower per capita income, it would be inappropriate to calculate their needs on an equal basis.

For the new Länder the German unity fund (*Fonds deutsche Einheit*) provides the main reallocation of funds that would otherwise have been allocated through the *Finanzausgleich*. This fund is to provide DM115bn to the new Länder over a period of four and a half years, with DM35bn in 1992, to be financed by the federal government (DM20bn) and from public credit raised on capital markets (DM95bn). The resultant debt burden is shared equally between the federal government and the old

Länder, and the funds raised are allocated among the new Länder on the basis of their populations.

In addition to the direct transfers there are payments for social security provision, such as for unemployment and pensions, which in 1991 amounted to a net transfer to the east of DM25.5bn. Transfers from the federal budget amounted to DM43.5bn in 1991. This included some DM22bn for the Treuhandanstalt. In total the financial transfers from the west to the east amounted to DM130.5bn in 1991 and DM160bn in 1992. These levels of expenditure are higher than were originally anticipated, in part because the initial expectations about tax revenue in the east have not been anywhere near fulfilled, owing to the sharp decline in industrial and economic output. At one stage it was expected that the east would generate about half the level of tax revenue at the old FRG. But in reality the west is currently paying for more than 70% of the east's needs. The level of transfers is therefore high and rising. To make matters worse, most of the resources are going on social provisions, or income support schemes of different kinds for east Germans, rather than in investment for rebuilding the east German economy.

By the beginning of 1991 it had become clear that the initial calculations had been over-optimistic. Strenuous efforts were made to reduce public expenditure in the west. The subsidies provided to west German industry, especially in the coal industry, were a prime target. Belt-tightening also threatened to affect investment plans in such sectors as the German railways, which were in the middle of a modernization programme. Despite threatening to resign if his plans to reduce subsidies by DM30bn were not accepted, the then Economics Minister Jürgen Möllemann struggled to make an impression on expenditure. The first indications were apparent that west German workers were reluctant to pay the price – which in the case of the coal miners would probably be unemployment – for the provision of social support for east Germans.

The difficulties in reducing subsidies meant that much of the increased costs of unification had to be financed through an increase in public debt. The immediate costs of this were less obvious but in order to finance the higher debt interest rates drifted upwards. The Bundesbank became uneasy with the state of public finances and pursued a tight monetary policy in order to prevent the increase in credit resulting in inflation rising above 4–5%.

Despite Chancellor Kohl's assurances to the contrary during the 1990 election campaign, tax increases were introduced in July 1991, supposedly on a temporary basis to reduce the level of public debt and the fiscal deficit; they were justified by the high cost of financing the Gulf crisis and giving aid to the Soviet Union.[13] The tax measures themselves were an important step towards meeting convergence criteria required to satisfy the conditions for German participation in EMU and the ultimate adoption of a single currency. They were to go hand in hand with a redoubling of the efforts to introduce a market economy in the east, so that subsidies could be reduced and tax revenue increased. In order to contain inflationary pressures created by the growth in public borrowing, the government called for a zero wage round, i.e. no wage increases.

These measures adversely affected the government's popularity. Trade unions, in particular, were not prepared to accept a zero wage round while facing significant tax increases. They argued that in effect the costs of unification were being shifted onto those who could least afford them, and in any case the government had clearly broken its election promise on taxes. The financial burden of unification was clearly creating tensions throughout west German society and disrupting the relatively stable patterns of redistribution. The public sector workers' union led the fight against the government over the wage round with its first strike in 18 years. This was ended with a settlement of a package amounting to an average increase of 5.4% – exceeding the government negotiators' offer, but apparently low enough to avoid nervousness in financial markets about the future prospects for inflation.

The impact on the EC
Just as reallocation within Germany has sought to maintain a social consensus, so within the Community the provision of structural funds has sought to promote cohesion within the Community. The FRG has financed the major direct costs of unification from domestic sources and funds, including borrowing.[14] The Community's contribution (3bn ecus) was more a gesture of solidarity. The increase in EC expenditures on agriculture as a result of the inclusion of the GDR in the CAP has not required any reassessment of the total budget.

In future it seems likely that significant parts of the new Länder will, according to the per capita income criteria, become eligible for EC structural fund support. In his speech introducing the Commission's programme for 1992 and in particular the proposals for the so-called Delors II package on the future financing of the Community, Commission President Delors argued that the EC 'must show a clear sign of its solidarity with the great task of reconstruction which has to date been largely carried by the federal German government'.[15] This shows that the integration of the GDR into the EC is not a closed chapter as far as the provision of Community financial support is concerned.

Having waived any claims on EC structural funds in 1990, the FRG government could be seen as in a sense renegotiating the terms of accession of the GDR, should it now claim a case for the eastern Länder receiving funds under the next EC structural fund programme. The main impact of the financial costs of unification on the Community will not be the pressure to renegotiate on structural funds; it will be a reduced ability or willingness on the part of Germany to make increased contributions to the EC budget. This is important at a time when the Community is negotiating the Delors II package. It will also be of considerable importance for Britain, because it severely reduces the likelihood of Britain retaining the repayments it managed to negotiate in the first Delors package of 1988.

Conclusions

Faced with the uncertainties of unification, decision-makers have tended to opt for caution. This has meant that, with some minor exceptions, unification has not been used as a means of bringing about change in the German system. The *Ordnungspolitik* based on competitive market structures is at best open to flexible interpretation. It is at present too early to say whether the social consensus will be significantly affected, or whether the east German population will have the same understanding of what it entails.

As for the operation of the Treuhand, pressures for a more active industrial/structural policy remain, and if it is possible to conclude anything yet it is that the experience of unification has helped to contribute to a genuine debate in Germany about the merits of an active industrial policy.

The EC has not played an active role in the restructuring process. For the present, the Commission has given the Treuhand a relatively free hand to go about the task of privatization.

In the short term the impact of unification on the overall position of German industry has been to weaken it rather than to strengthen it, and there is no suggestion that Germany will become an *économie dominante*. But the picture in the longer term may be different; indeed the official German line is that the difficulties industry is currently facing will pay off in the end, only the time span being uncertain. German companies have incurred considerable costs in investing in the east and in return they have extended their strength to cover the whole German market. With some minor exceptions, foreign competitors have not succeeded in using unification to gain footholds in the German market in important strategic sectors. This means that the existing German 'sacred cows', such as the regulation of the energy markets, have become more rather than less sacred as a result of unification. In some areas this will make the task of creating a single European market harder, not easier.

6
CASE-STUDY: FINANCIAL SERVICES

This case-study focuses particularly on banking and insurance, since these are considered to be a high priority interest from a British point of view. It is widely accepted that the German financial services market is relatively closed. For potential investors in the new Länder, access to the distribution networks was vital if they were to reach both the newly emerging market and Germany as a whole. Given that Germany has such a central role to play in the European single market, any dominance by German companies in such strategic sectors could only delay the liberalization process and thus endanger the smooth functioning of the markets.

Banking

The development of a two-tier system in the GDR, 1989–90
In 1989 the Modrow administration took the first steps to reform the banking sector in the GDR, recognizing the need to escape the dominance of the Staatsbank if a modern, two-tier banking system was to be established. There were only six different credit institutions in the GDR,[1] as compared with over 4,000 in the FRG. For the customer, this generally meant that only one type of bank account was available, with a fixed interest rate on savings.

Once the decision had been taken to introduce the Deutschmark into east Germany, the restructuring process had to be speeded up considerably. Following the introduction of new Staatsbank legislation in April 1990, savings banks and commercial banks became independent. This was not achieved by setting up individual credit institutions, but rather by a consolidation of the association of existing ones in accordance with the west German model. The newly-formed Deutsche Kreditbank (Ost) inherited the commercial activities of the former Staatsbank as a joint-stock corporation. This action was to prove crucial in determining the eventual structure of the industry.

Three joint ventures were then set up with Deutsche Bank, the Dresdner Bank and the Verkehrskreditbank – all corporations based on cash subscriptions with none of the old lending business. Both elements worked together in the same branch, one taking care of old business, the other of new, with the old debt remaining for the most part in the hands of the Deutsche Kreditbank AG. On 2 July 1990 the Kreditbank was privatized and west German banks were free to set up their own branches in the east; they were now able to consolidate the position they had established under the Kreditbank's umbrella. The Deutsche and Dresdner inherited both branches and customers from the Staatsbank in 1990 in return for fees to cover the administration of old loans.

Developments since unification

The opportunity for foreign credit institutions to gain access to the market did not arise until after unification, when the GDR took on the *acquis communautaire* without any derogations in the financial services sector, as well as accepting both incoming and proposed single market legislation. Few firms actually took the opportunity. One reason may have been the lack of export financing business.[2] In Germany this is normally undertaken by banks, with the government offering export credit guarantees through the Hermes scheme. It is noteworthy, however, that whereas the total volume of business in Germany rose by only 8% as a result of unification, for banks it rose by as much 18% – a fact that clearly illustrates the extent to which west German banks had already captured the market. The three largest – Deutsche, Dresdner and Commerzbank – have between them secured a total of 75% of the east German market. This trend to oligopoly, as well as the tendency of east German customers to favour the traditional savings banks (*Sparkassen*), which hold 80% of accounts (compared with 52% in west Germany), has serious implications for competition at the European level.

In these circumstances, it is quite understandable that Germany's EC partners expressed some concern that unification had resulted in market dominance by the large west German banking and insurance companies. On the other hand, there was no doubting the urgent need to establish a sound banking and insurance system in the region in order to attract the capital necessary to match the massive investment requirements. In the event this meant that strict adherence to FRG and EC competition rules would not have been practicable, even had the legislation actually applied in the GDR at that time.[3] In view of the degree of concentration of credit institutions in the GDR prior to the restructuring, as well as the need to shorten dramatically an otherwise lengthy process, the outcome was acceptable to the authorities concerned. The *Amt für Wettbewerbsschutz* had virtually no leverage.[4] Officials in the Commission also had little opportunity to affect the structure of the sector; for example, when the joint venture between Deutsche Bank and the Deutsche Kreditbank (2 April 1990) was referred to them for consideration of its impact on competition and trade within the Community, they accepted the outcome, since a previous restriction giving the Kreditbank a monopoly on loans to industry had been lifted and the Deutsche Bank had allowed competitors to acquire substantial shares in Kreditbank's subsidiaries. It is unclear to what extent this was because of the legal vacuum created by action taken 'as if' the GDR were part of the EC.[5]

A potential bone of contention among Germany's competitors, should the practice continue on a long-term basis, is the level of guarantees extended by the Treuhandanstalt to cover bank loans to East German companies undergoing restructuring. This has turned them into government assets, in addition to which Deutsche and Dresdner receive a fee for administering loans from the Staatsbank. This is effectively risk-free business, making penetration of the loans market by outsiders extremely difficult. The absence of traditional opening balance sheets has made German banks reluctant to accept loans at a company's own risk, particularly since German banks by tradition lend against assets as opposed to cash flow projections.[6] The level of own-risk lending has increased slightly since unification, but this has been mainly where the loans are backed by major west German shareholders.

Initially the THA credits were seen as a temporary measure. Once it became clear, however, that the Treuhand expected to continue its activities for much longer than anticipated, it was actively seeking to remove such guarantees by the end of 1992, in order to be seen to support foreign investors (and because of the high costs involved). Instead it proposes to borrow directly, thereby offering considerable savings to the German taxpayer by servicing the debts at a more favourable rate of interest. The banks have been sceptical, since only about 20% of the companies which the Treuhand has on its books were expected to be able to produce balance sheets for 1991. The Treuhand also intends to increase the number of management buy-outs by selling companies at a reduced price in return for employment guarantees, or by financing the buy-outs through either industrial partnerships or foreign portfolios.[7] Such steps could well increase the role of foreign banks in the region.

Insurance: Allianz and Staatliche Versicherung

In March 1990 the East German Council of Ministers decided to dissolve Staatliche Versicherung der DDR, the state monopoly over insurance services, and it was put under the administration of the Treuhandanstalt. On 1 May the east German Deutsche Versicherung AG (DV) was established as a joint venture between the Treuhand (49%) and Allianz Versicherung (51%, acquired for DM270.74m). The agreed share capital was 1bn Ostmarks, with capital reserves of DM61.7m. It offered non-life insurance, third party liability and staff insurance (i.e. under pension schemes), just as Staatliche Versicherung had done. Allianz was able to offer DV the capital, systems and know-how necessary to make it a modern and competitive insurance operation.

Allianz is the biggest insurance company in the EC; it has 223 companies in 45 countries, with 23 west German units accounting for some 40% of its total premium income. Purchases of foreign companies during the 1980s have made Allianz unique in its degree of internationalization, 44% of its income now coming from abroad. Worldwide group premium income jumped by 8.9% between 1988 and 1989, from DM29.2bn to DM31.8bn, and consolidated net group profits totalled DM1.6bn in 1989.

The west German Cartel Office believed that the Allianz deal fell foul of Article 86 of the EEC Treaty by reinforcing Allianz's dominant position in the west German market. Helmut Haussmann, the then west German Economics Minister, took special action to try to block the move. As we have already seen, however, the powers of both the Cartel Office and the EC were severely limited since the GDR remained outside both FRG and EC jurisdiction until October 1990.

Following discussions with the THA and the Cartel Office, the European Commission was satisfied that there was insufficient evidence that Allianz had abused its dominant market position.[8] Account was taken of the fact that Allianz had been asked to lend its know-how to create a new structure and it seemed reasonable to believe that the intention had not been to create a monopoly for itself. Allianz undertook to invest some DM2bn in the new Bundesländer and expected initial losses. The bid also included certain employment protection measures. Allianz was of course prepared to take on such losses, since it was not the value of the individual policies of the DV which gave it its intrinsic value, but the access to a major *distribution channel.*

Two factors influenced the EC and west German competition authorities. First, rights were granted to policyholders who had existing contracts with Staatliche Versicherung to terminate their policies if they so wished. Second, the east German insurance market was open to new entrants and therefore it would not be possible for Allianz to maintain a dominant market position. The Commission was satisfied that both domestic and foreign competition would be possible, and the Cartel Office subsequently withdrew its opposition to the merger. Had the EC Merger Control Regulation been in force at that time, the outcome would very likely have been the same.

It has been estimated that the Allianz contract signed with the Treuhand amounted to a cost of around DM6bn to the German taxpayer, because it was purchased without historic exposure (although this figure is probably excessive).[9] The insurance contracts made with the Staatliche Versicherung (some of which were for twenty years) attracted premiums at one-third of the rate demanded in the former FRG. Even though there were more restrictions on claims than would apply under a typical west German contract, any claims which fell due had to be paid for, and these ultimately became the liability of the German government, since the Treuhand still had a 49% share and was responsible for former GDR liabilities. The former Staatliche Versicherung, as a division of the Ministry of Finance, had collected premium incomes and paid out on claims as part of the ministry's budget. Thus unlike in a private insurance company there was no explicit reserve fund allocated to settling unexpired risks or outstanding claims. The Treuhand and Allianz subsequently agreed that any outstanding claims arising on premiums paid before 30 June 1990 would remain the responsibility of the ministry which had collected them, and thereafter the responsibility of the Treuhand under a separate legal entity. Estimates of the exact amount likely to be involved are yet to be confirmed. In any event, the Finance Ministry made some DM1.5bn available from its budget for this purpose.

Both German and foreign competitors of Allianz continued to believe that the Allianz deal had excluded them. A group of six, including Colonia (Germany's second-largest insurance company) and Gothaer, had made an alternative cash offer to the Treuhand for a 51% stake in DV. The plan involved breaking up the state monopoly into five regional groups, but the Treuhand argued that any economies of scale would be

75

lost because the east German population was relatively small. Notably the offer did not include a higher price.

By June 1991 accusations were being made that the deal had in fact been underpriced, by as much as DM2bn.[10] The Treuhand contended that the central handling of the deal had been conducted by the former GDR Finance Ministry and that the sale had been concluded by Hans Modrow personally. The THA personnel could therefore not be accused of collusion to obtain Staatliche Versicherung below its market value. The Treuhand further argued that it had sold DV to the 'highest bidder', and that this had had to take into account such factors as committed investment and employment guarantees. Such considerations have subsequently become an important factor in the EC's assessment of the 'playing-field'.

Start-up losses for Allianz arising from the DV deal were huge – DM500m for the second half of 1990 alone. Allianz now has 20–30% of market share in the new Bundesländer. DV employs some 14,000 staff who generate only DM2bn in premium income, compared with the DM10bn generated by 20,000 staff in west Germany. Allianz has estimated it will require five years to break even and although it expects the insurance market in the new Länder to expand in the next ten years or so, it remains sceptical about the possible volume increases that might be involved.

In August 1991 Allianz entered into talks with the Treuhand regarding the purchase of the remaining 49% of the shares. Initial industry estimates valued the shares at DM270m,[11] but the price eventually agreed was DM440m.

British involvement in the sector

No British banking or insurance company was involved in any of these acquisitions. This was not surprising, given that German firms would in any event always have had the edge in terms of location and common language. Such factors are extremely important in a sector heavily reliant on personal customer contact. Allianz was also able to exploit its financial largesse and to sustain losses over a fairly long period without a theat to existing business. In contrast, British companies are increasingly under pressure to make short-term returns on investments.

Within the British insurance sector there was general agreement that the Allianz deal had been an attempt to exclude competitors. Nonetheless, as consumers showed their preferences by moving their policies away from what is still regarded by many as a state monopoly, it became increasingly clear that the market would be very much open. However, there was very little new business on offer since those large companies in joint ventures with west German firms had simply to extend existing policies. Of much greater interest to the British is the development of the still insignficant life assurance market, because it is far less dependent upon personal contacts.

British banks are represented in the former FRG in personal banking services, in the credit card market and in the futures and options exchanges. Barclays Bank has been involved in Germany for many years and since unification has opened a service centre in East Berlin for the new eastern market. Barclays de Zoete Wedd (BZW) has become a full member of the Deutsche Terminbörse (DTB), the Frankfurt-based options and futures exchange. Barclays has also acquired Merck Finck, one of Germany's oldest and most distinguished private banks, and reached an agreement with the retailer Hertie to sell financial services through its stores, thus gaining a foothold in the German credit card market.[12] Early evidence suggests that the citizens of the new Länder have just as great a propensity to save as the west Germans, but the high level of unemployment and bankruptcies in the region means that the area is potentially a very high risk. Barclays has, however, found a less risky niche in its operations in industry leasing, thereby assisting the re-equipment of industry.

None of the British banks involved in Germany have any real involvement in retailing, residential mortgage financing or consumer lending, which accounts for 95% of the market in the five new Länder. Although the Treuhand has welcomed non-west German financial investors, small consumers have tended to favour the more well-known local companies.

British firms do not expect that EC financial services directives will translate into the immediate removal of all obstacles to market entry, but they do believe that continental European markets will become easier to penetrate.[13] The German market is regarded as particularly attractive because of its size and wealth. In the case of pension fund management, life assurance and certain banking and securities products, many British firms feel they have a superior product to those of German companies. In practice, however, there are major obstacles to foreign penetration of these markets, such as the German corporate shareholding structures, long-established banking relationships, local market practices and the conservative approach of consumers. This has deterred potential British investors, who have seen better opportunities for a higher return elsewhere in Europe.

Conclusions

The rapid transformation of the centrally planned banking and insurance sector in the former GDR into a competitive market system was vital to a successful restructuring of the economy. In spite of the west German market's competitiveness, it has nonetheless remained closed to outside competitors for the reasons outlined above. The immediate impact of unification appears to have been further concentration of the German banking and insurance business towards the big players. Furthermore, the changes in the financial system in the former GDR have enlarged the already exceptionally large-scale public credit sector in the FRG. It is still too early to assess how this situation will change, especially once the single market is operational. Nonetheless, given that Germany is the largest European economy, if potential inroads into its market as a result of unification fail to materialize, it is difficult to see how the benefits promised to consumers after 1993 can be realized.

7

CASE-STUDY: THE ENERGY SECTOR

The unification of Germany coincided with attempts by the EC to liberalize European gas and electricity markets, attempts which had been greeted with general scepticism. This case-study examines the restructuring of the energy sector in the GDR and considers how policy-makers dealt with the competing needs of attracting the necessary investment and preventing market dominance. It also considers the effectiveness of foreign bidders and whether there was a preference for German companies, as well as the likely long-term effects on the power market in Europe.

Coal and nuclear power were early focuses of EC attention, but neither the EEC Treaty nor the Single European Act (SEA) made explicit provision for a comprehensive energy policy. Implicitly Article 8A of the SEA did touch the energy sector, with its more general proposals for the harmonization of taxation, recognition of standards and the liberalization of procurement. In this way it challenged the general acceptance that utilities be treated as 'natural monopolies' in return for the guaranteed provision of certain services and investment obligations.[1] Attempts to extend the internal market to energy, for both products and services, have been under way since 1988, with an initial focus on the very important gas and electricity markets.[2] The aim is to break the close links between production, distribution and transmission and thus make European energy markets more efficient (through envisaged economies of scale) and increase competition, as barriers to trade are removed.[3] The most controversial proposal is to open up the European gas and electricity grids to third parties. Notwithstanding the importance of these liberalization objectives, EC environmental policy, in particular the goal of stabilizing carbon dioxide emissions at 1990 levels by the year 2000, was also to have an impact on investment decisions in the new Bundesländer.[4]

The electricity sector in the former FRG

In the old FRG, EC proposals had met strong resistance from the 'power cartel' – the major electricity generation and supply companies, the sub-contractors, power generators, and employers and trade unions representing the coal industry. The public electricity supply is highly concentrated, dominated by eight vertically integrated companies. Hard coal (anthracite) is heavily subsidized by both the Federal and Länder governments, directly via the *Kohlepfennig* (a price levy of approximately 3.5% on electricity accounts) and indirectly via the *Jahrhundertvertrag*. This was an agreement signed in 1980 between the coal mining industry and the power generators to increase the supply of coal from 33m tonnes in 1981 to 45m in 1995. This has kept down Germany's net power imports, even though high extraction costs make hard coal uncompetitive. Three factors have led to increasing criticism of this policy: the slowdown in energy use during the early 1980s, the much lower cost of imported coal, and the increased use of nuclear power. The rise in total energy consumption during the 1980s was increasingly satisfied by lignite (which is cheaper to extract than hard coal) and by nuclear power. Attempts by the federal government to abolish the *Kohlepfennig* have so far been largely futile. At the Länder level reforms have been opposed on both regional and social policy grounds (envisaged loss of income, tax revenues and employment in areas where the local unemployment rate is often double the national average).

In response to pressure from both domestic and industrial users, as well as the European Commission, a German Committee of Independent Experts was set up in 1987[5] to consider ways of dismantling anti-competitive practices. The Committee rejected the argument that electricity was a special case; its view (fully supported by the then Economics Minister, Jürgen Möllemann) was that the massive public intervention in the industry significantly contravened competition laws. In response Germany's suppliers have argued that electricity imported from France is cheaper only because nuclear energy is in their view unfairly subsidized by the French government. Thus any proposed reforms to 'level the playing-field' would have to take account of these different starting-points.

In such a sensitive area, many politicians have been reluctant to question the status quo, though Möllemann was a notable exception. The costs of unification, together with pressure to reduce state subsidies, offered an opportunity to implement unpopular measures (such as running down the domestic hard coal industry) without provoking a head-on clash with the trade unions, as happened under the Thatcher administration in Britain in 1983. For the EC, unification offered a chance of breaking up the power cartel by attracting foreign investors into the new Bundesländer and thereby opening up the German market as a whole to competition.

The energy sector in the former GDR

Energy resources

A number of problems faced the energy sector in the former GDR at the time of unification: supply bottlenecks; low energy efficiency; serious environmental pollution; heavy dependence for all mineral resources (except lignite) on imports, most of which came from the former USSR.[6]

The eastern part of Germany is poor in natural energy resources. In 1990 reserves were estimated at only 100,000 tonnes of recoverable mineral oil and 45bn cubic metres (BCM) of poor-quality natural gas (compared with 96 BCM in 1975),[7] enough for only four more years at current rates of consumption. Hard coal seams had been exhausted during the 1970s. However, reserves of lignite of low calorific content totalled 23,460m tonnes in 1990 and were the fifth largest in the world. Consumption of lignite was the highest in the world – 309m tonnes in 1987, over 80% of energy production. Per capita consumption of energy prior to unification was 25% higher than in west Germany. Power stations emitted over five million tonnes of sulphur per annum and twenty-five times more carbon dioxide than in the Federal Republic – the highest level of per capita emissions in the world.[8]

As the EC environmental derogations negotiated with the EC expire at the end of 1995, replacement fuels for lignite have to be found, especially for domestic heating. This is most likely to be oil in the short term. Power stations could continue to be fuelled by lignite if fluidized gas desulphurization (FGD) retrofits are installed, although it is uneconomical in small power stations. Natural gas, as a cleaner fuel, is likely to be used much more in the medium to long run, since OECD (International Energy Authority) rules forbid the construction of new oil-fired stations and domestic hard coal is uncompetitive. In the 1990s it is likely that virtually all new fossil fuel power stations in the rest of the EC will be fired by gas.

However, the west German trade union organization (DGB) strongly opposes any shift away from domestic hard coal use in power stations. It also shared the wider public antipathy to the construction of new nuclear power plants in the new Länder, wanting on the contrary to see an overall reduction in nuclear fuels throughout Germany, again in line with public opinion.[9] Existing nuclear power installations in the GDR had to be shut down for safety reasons upon unification, though the supporters of nuclear power have argued for its environmental and cost advantages relative to hard coal.

Structure of the sector

The energy sector in the GDR was highly centralized and monopolistic.[10] It boasted an institutionalized energy-saving policy, albeit one that was almost impossible to implement, since consumers had virtually no control over their own consumption. Gas, electricity and heating fuels were supplied at the district level to both firms and private individuals by 15 large *Kombinate* (one for each administrative district). Responsibility for electricity production was separated from supply through the integrated grid system (*Verbundnetz*). The 'Modrow strategy' of 1989 proposed less use of lignite and more of hard coal and natural gas, and a reduction of state subsidies. As part of the reform process, Modrow ended the division of responsibility between production and utilities. This runs counter to the EC Commission's preference (on the grounds that it would restrict competition), and can be seen as a move towards the west German model.

In March 1990, when the Treuhandanstalt was established, it was given the task of identifying suitable Western partners for joint ventures. Following the formation of a coalition government under Lothar de Maizière in April, a further and more fundamental reform of the energy sector was introduced. The THA became part of the Economics Ministry, with the task of privatizing and restructuring some 180 enterprises in the energy sector alone. According to the minister responsible, Professor Steinberg, energy policy was already very similar to that of the FRG, where the large energy companies dominated the market.[11] This was in line with what many economics experts and politicians wanted.

The electricity supply contracts – Verbundvertrag

Any hopes that unification would provide an impetus for change were soon to be dashed. The three large west German power companies, RWE (*Rheinisch-Westfälische Elektrizitätswerke*), Preußenelektra and Bayernwerk, had already started negotiations with the former *Kombinate* directors and the GDR coalition government to purchase the entire electricity sector. Political groupings within the Volkskammer were meanwhile debating legislation to decentralize the sector in favour of the *Kommunen* (local authorities) and the Länder.

Indeed, the initial proposals by the GDR Ministry for Energy and Environment were to transfer both generation and supply rights to the 'big three', supposedly in the 'interest of security of supply'. This proposal was opposed by the Federal Cartel Office and others. Nonetheless the Cartel Office allowed the purchase to proceed provided that the *Kombinate*'s gas and power cartels were broken and that the big three's share holdings did not exceed 75%; the remaining 25% was to be offered to five west German utilities.

The Cartel Office also recommended that the agreement should not include the distribution business which belonged to the former *Bezirke* (district administrations) of Dresden, Halle, Schwerin and East Berlin.[12] This was to go instead to the other five west German companies, who had put in late bids. The *Verbundvertrag* was signed on 22 August 1990, as were contracts between the fifteen regional GDR energy supply companies (*Energieversorgungsunternehmen* – EVUs) and the west German EVUs[13] which, in return, committed them to a total investment of DM1.3bn. The agreement limited the commercial risk involved, and environmental liabilities were excluded.

The RWE–Preußenelektra–Bayernwerk consortium thus obtained a 75% share of 60% of the *Verbundnetz* – the 60% corresponding to its market share in west Germany. The Cartel Office had believed that the newly-created structure would open up competition because of the geographical location of the *Bezirke*'s markets, but this was limited by the Treuhand's stipulation (presumably with the backing of the Federal Economics Ministry) that the regional firms were obliged not only to purchase 70% of their energy needs from the newly constituted Verbundnetz AG, but to contract to do so for a minimum period of twenty years. The justification for this was the possible rehabilitation of economically viable lignite-fuelled power stations (although there are considerable doubts whether this would be feasible).[14] It is likely that other interests played a part – for example, the Treuhand's reluctance to contemplate immediate redundancies in the lignite sector, or an attempt to undermine the interests of the hard coal industry at a time when the government was already trying to break up the cartel so as to facilitate the introduction of foreign competition. Moreover, the Cartel Office's proposals would also have allowed firms to buy power where they wished and therefore would have impinged on the still unresolved debate about open access.[15] Indeed the Treuhand's stipulation might well have been made for no other reason than that without it the assets of the businesses covered by the *Verbundvertrag* would have been far smaller and it was extremely important to attract private investment into the region. As the lignite stations are phased out, a 'renegotiation' of the agreement can be expected, probably before twenty years have elapsed.

The conflict between the Verbundvertrag and the Volkskammer

The Volkskammer was keen to assign responsibility for local power supply to the local authorities, under the management of the *Stadtwerke* (municipal services for the utilities), as was a constitutional right in the Federal Republic of Germany. Electricity and gas supplies are used to cross-subsidize less profitable municipal services, such as public transport. To secure this right a law was passed on 17 May 1990 stipulating that the local authorities should be responsible for the supply of mains-connected power, and that the state-owned assets should be transferred to them. This contradicted the substance of de Maizière's negotiations with the three west German EVUs for the purchase of the entire electricity sector. In the end the *Stadtwerke* were entitled only to shares in the legal successors of the former *Kombinate*, to a maximum of 49%.

Some provisions of the treaty of unification also conflicted with the west German property ownership law, which entitled the *Stadtwerke* to a 15% share of the assets. Eventually there was agreement between the Treuhand, the big three west German power companies and the East German municipalities, allowing *Stadtwerke* to be classified separately. The *Verbundvertrag* had transferred the assets to the electricity supply companies and the *Stadtwerke* were to approach these firms if they wished to take over the administration of the electricity supply. In each case the negotiations were to be carried out directly with the regional power companies, on condition that security of supply and price competitiveness criteria could be met. Nonetheless over 160 former *Stadtwerke* have initiated proceedings against the Treuhand.[16] This will have a significant impact on the type of fuel used for power generation in each region.

Critics of the Verbundvertrag

Outside observers have criticized the electricity contracts for their lack of transparency, in the light of the negotiations which took place behind the scenes. Only a month before the agreement was signed, EC Competition Commissioner Sir Leon Brittan had received assurances that GDR mergers and takeovers would be treated as if EEC Treaty provisions applied (in this case Articles 85 and 86 and the Merger Control Regulation) and that maximum transparency would be provided. It was further agreed to establish direct contact between the competition directorate (DGIV) and the GDR's *Amt für Wettbewerbsschutz*.

Both the west German Economics Minister at the time, Helmut Haussmann, and the head of the AfW, Reinhold Wutzke, were strong critics nonetheless. Haussmann believed that the AfW should have accepted west German cartel legislation after GEMSU came into force on 1 July 1990.[17]

The gas sector

Conscious of criticism of the *Verbundvertrag*, the THA wanted to ensure that the disposal of the newly-formed supra-regional gas transmission company, *Verbundnetzgas* (VNG), complied fully with EC competition law. It was keen to persuade non-German gas producers and transmission companies to acquire holdings in VNG. The final share distribution was to be as follows:

Elf Acquitaine	5%
Statoil	5%
Gazprom	5%
Gommern	5%
Municipalities	15% – 1 share
Wintershall	15% + 1 share
Ruhrgas	35%
BEB	10%
British Gas	5%[18]

The distribution was very carefully thought through, given the possibility of pressure from Ruhrgas and the municipalities combined. Ruhrgas already enjoyed a dominant market position in west Germany and a near-monopoly over Soviet gas imports. The Federal Cartel Office allowed the deal to proceed because the Treuhand sold the majority share to companies and district bodies which were not legally and economically dependent upon Ruhrgas.[19] Nonetheless other bidders objected to the combined Ruhrgas and BEB share, which would give them 45% block power, and duly filed with the Commission a formal request for an investigation to ascertain whether Ruhrgas's acquisition fell foul of Article 86 (abuse of dominant market position). This was a historic move since the EC had never before actually used this article against an energy utility. Some doubts remain as to whether the case falls under national or EC competence, given that gas pipelines are national networks but the European links cross national boundaries.[20]

In terms of market access, the Ruhrgas acquisition was a clear pre-emptive strike. VNG, formed from the former GDR 'gas grid' supply distributor, was sole owner of the transmission network, and controlled all deliveries of imported natural gas. But since the former supplier had been wound up, VNG would lack the finance to set up a natural gas network single-handed. The three types of gas – natural gas of high calorific value imported from the USSR, low calorific value Salzwedel gas and town gas (from lignite) – were distributed via three different, incompatible systems. It is likely that both Salzwedel and town gas will ultimately be replaced by natural gas, for reasons of both safety and economies of scale, with a doubling of consumption expected by the year 2000. The race to link up with new supply sources has already begun, particularly in eastern Europe, in an attempt to reduce dependence on the former Soviet Union (the CIS). Potential investors, including British Gas, are therefore keen to gain a foothold in the new Länder.

Disappointed at their respective share allocations in VNG, Wintershall and Gazprom (the former Soviet gas ministry) joined forces to form WIEH (Wintershall Erdgas Handelshaus GmbH) to market gas in the eastern part of Germany. The joint venture effectively gave Wintershall control over gas delivered via Orenburg into east Germany. WIEH is building a new pipeline through Saxony and Thuringia running from the Czech border to Hessen, more or less parallel to the existing STEGAL (Sachsen-Thüringen Erdgasleitung), which is a high-pressure gas pipeline, also built by WIEH. This would compete with the VNG/Essener Ruhrgas project already under construction, to allow the input of both Soviet and, more importantly, North Sea gas. These projects will be crucial in determining future competition in the gas market.

The gas price dispute

The battle for control of the East German gas industry has resulted in a public dispute between Ruhrgas and WIEH over the price of gas charged to VNG, but the real issue is one of control of Russian gas supplies to eastern Germany. Wintershall is owned by BASF, which, with assets of

Figure 7.1 Russian natural gas supplies to Germany

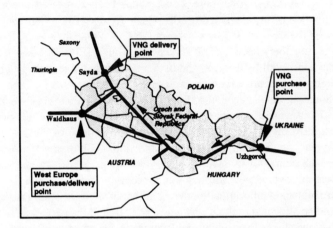

Source: Gas Matters 1992. Reproduced by kind permission of EconoMatters.

some DM45bn, is about four times bigger than Ruhrgas, using some 2bn cubic metres of natural gas per year. Ruhrgas had, prior to unification, enjoyed a monopoly over Soviet gas imports in west Germany and a dominant position in the gas industry as a whole. As a major chemical company and buyer of gas, BASF had always argued that Ruhrgas's prices were too high and had decided to try to import gas itself from the North Sea via Kassel to Ludwigshafen using Gazprom;[21] it has sought to sell this gas to other users.

An unusual feature of Soviet/GDR gas agreements was the annual negotiation of volumes and prices on a barter/clearing rouble basis, according to the CMEA five-year average formula. The Orenburg contract became the property of the Federal Government upon unification and was then assigned to VNG upon purchase, but this was contested by Wintershall. VNG signed an agreement in 1991 with Soyuzgazexport, (the export division of Gazprom), on Yamburg volumes, whereas Gazprom assigned the Orenburg volumes exclusively to WIEH to sell.

The Soviet Union exported gas to west Germany with Ruhrgas paying a cost insurance freight (c.i.f.) price at Waidhaus; the GDR in contrast bought gas at Uzhgorod on the Ukrainian border and took responsibility for transit (see Fig. 7.1). Since WIEH charged at Uzhgorod (i.e. without transport) the same price as Gazprom charged its customers at Waidhaus, VNG have argued that the price of the gas via Sayda is 20% higher than that via Waidhaus, because of the additional transit costs through Czechoslovakia. Furthermore, concern has been expressed about the distribution of the estimated profits which go to WIEH, where they are split on the basis of 85% to Gazprom, 15% to Wintershall, even though both companies have a 50% shareholding in WIEH. This has led to allegations, both by Ruhrgas and by VNG (in which Ruhrgas is a major shareholder), of price fixing by WIEH.[22]

Since natural gas accounted for only 8.7% of primary energy use in the new Länder in 1990, with no significant rise in demand expected before the turn of the century, the dispute is more symbolic of the battle for supremacy in the German gas market than important in price terms.

In the course of its investigations over the price dispute, the Cartel Office discovered new information concerning the VNG privatization. The Treuhand had originally envisaged that 30% of the Ruhrgas shares would be allocated to the *Kommunen*. They lacked the necessary capital to buy the shares themselves and Ruhrgas had stepped in with offers of financial assistance. The offer was upheld after the Treuhand finally decided to reduce these share holdings to 15%. Eventually the share allocation of the 14 towns and cities was bundled together in a new organization, which signed a loan agreement with Ruhrgas. The Cartel Office was very concerned about the provision that interest payments (at prevailing market rates) would be deferred until such time as the first profits were recorded, considering this a threat to the independence of the *Kommunen*, and fearing a possible impact on the *Stadtwerke*. Moreover, the deferral agreement had not been notified to the Cartel Office and apparently had come to light only by chance – another case of lack of transparency. In its investigation of the Ruhrgas and BEB share allocations in VNG, the Cartel Office vetoed the credit agreement and made a proviso that any further applications for shares in VNG must not be from companies legally and/or economically dependent upon Ruhrgas/BEB. A new loan agreement has subsequently been concluded, more or less on the same terms, with the Bayerische Landesbank.

The EC dimension

EC policy-makers took the view that the restructuring of the energy sector in the new Bundesländer should be implemented in accordance with both Community competition rules and wider energy policy objectives and environmental standards (with some derogations until 1996). However, unification has done nothing to ease the passage of the electricity and gas transit directives. Both concern grid-to-grid transactions and explicitly exclude reference to common carriage and third party access,[23] and there has been active resistance to EC regulatory control, especially in the gas sector.

Unlike Germany, Britain has specific regulatory bodies for the gas and electricity industries, although many would argue that the generator duopoly provides no real competition despite the spot pricing and independent grid regime. Nonetheless the obligation on the distributors in the new Bundesländer to take 70% of their requirements from the *Verbundnetz* has indisputably impaired competition in the short term. The continued support for the use of lignite in power stations could weaken the power cartel and therefore promote liberalization in the long term, but this remains to be seen. In 1991 Sir Leon Brittan presented a wide-ranging draft directive, covering access to the gas and electricity transmission infrastructure. His colleagues Martin Bangemann and Peter Schmidhuber were against the plans, which they believed would distort competition. As Germany is less reliant upon nuclear power than France, the Germans believe any 'squeezing out' of the coal industry might put them at a competitive disadvantage, by allowing Electricité de France easy access to their market, which they would not be able to reciprocate.

The Germans are not alone in fearing that the proposals risk opening up the more lucrative business to foreign competitors whilst smaller customers would suffer in terms of higher prices. It is doubtful whether the revised text agreed by the Commission in January 1992 can be implemented in its present form by 1993, even though it has been scaled down from Brittan's more ambitious proposals. Indeed, supporters of further liberalization in the gas and electricity sectors suffered a further setback in May 1992. At a meeting of EC Ministers and Heads of State only the UK, Denmark and Portugal supported Cardoso E Cunha's concept of a gradual opening up of the market by 1998. In the second phase, due to start in 1993, certain large industrial users would gain unrestricted access to the network. In the final phase, between 1996 and 1998, only private households and small industrial users would be excluded. Both France and the southern Mediterranean countries expressed reservations about even the second phase. Germany was more concerned about the means and speed of liberalization rather than the process itself.[24]

The EC decision to revoke a 1975 Directive which had restricted the use of natural gas in power stations will have an impact on the restructuring in eastern Germany. It is likely to encourage more gas to come on-stream and therefore could discourage investment in retrofitting lignite-fuelled power stations, with all the implications this has for the future of the lignite industry and the pricing structure.[25] British Gas recognized at a very early stage the viability of natural gas for the region and acted speedily to gain a foothold in what had been a natural monopoly.

Neither lignite nor nuclear energy is an ideal replacement for hard coal, even if they are perhaps cheaper. If lignite oxidizing plants were to be used without FGD retrofits, environmental damage would contradict both German and European environmental policy. However, FGDs are extremely expensive and few exist outside the US, Japan and Germany. The alternative, nuclear power, would be politically unacceptable.

Given the alternative fuels now available, it will be much harder to justify the *Jahrhundertvertrag* by reference to the exemption clause of Article 85(3) of the Treaty of Rome. The Commission believes the arguments that it secures supply to be exaggerated and recommends a maximum 20% of electricity production reserves for domestic use. It had sanctioned a limited exemption until 31 March 1991 and in May 1991 notified Bonn that it would seek the abolition of the *Kohlepfennig* by the end of 1993. In response, the German Coal Mining Association warned the government that alternative sources of state funding would be needed to prevent the industry collapsing. This conflict has yet to be resolved.

Conclusion

The restructuring of the energy sector in the GDR was a struggle for market dominance, with EC environmental policy probably having a more direct impact than its single market objectives. The sector was seen by both west German and foreign investors as one of the plum investments on offer in the region and demand for shares in the new companies was high. In the event, the influence of the west German power companies could not be resisted. In the case of gas, although the shares were more widely allocated, domination by west German companies meant a missed opportunity to strongly boost competition. As yet no clear benefits for small consumers have emerged. The pursuit of wider political goals rather than competition – especially environmental objectives and the need for massive investment – has superimposed the west German structure onto the new Bundesländer.

8

CASE-STUDY: AGRICULTURE

For the east German agricultural sector, unification meant above all integration into the EC's Common Agricultural Policy (CAP). The CAP is a crucial factor in determining both intra-Community relations and extra-Community trade agreements. The difficulties of integration are likely to have an important impact on the costs of implementing the CAP, and on the distribution of expenditure among member states, especially on the balance of contributions between France and Germany. This case-study will consider the two-way impact of unification on the CAP (particularly in the context of the reforms associated with the Uruguay Round of the GATT) and of the Community on the agricultural sector, not only in the new Länder but throughout Germany.

The agricultural sector in the former GDR

Organizational structure
The area of agricultural land in the GDR, approximately 6.26m hectares, was managed predominantly by agricultural production cooperatives (*Landwirtschaftliche Produktionsgenossenschaften*, LPG) and state-owned estates (*Volkseigene Güter*, VEG), on the basis of non-private owner-ship. LPGs were formed by the amalgamation of members' land and property. In legal terms land remained under private ownership but the right of use was transferred to the LPGs.

The preferred size of agricultural units was large, in keeping with the model favoured by the SED government. Highly specialized monocultural units were organized on industrial lines and run on an autarkic basis (see

Table 8.1). One of the government's main objectives was to introduce industrial methods of production into the agricultural sector as part of a drive towards a self-sufficient economy. This drive encouraged use of inappropriate land for agricultural production: about 20% of the region's soil is of poor quality (sandy and light). Logistic and environmental problems, coupled with the separation of crop and livestock production, meant that the system was inefficient. Although large farms with good soil were potentially viable, farming methods and farming stock, which have been starved of investment capital, will require huge sums to match west German standards.

Table 8.1 Area and number of agricultural holdings

	GDR	FRG	UK	EC12
Total area (m. hectares)	6.182	11.843	16.75	115.399
Arable land (m. hectares)	4.576	7.257	6.94	63.249
Number of agricultural holdings (thousands)	4.751	705	260	8,644
Size of holding (hectares)	4,500*	16.8	64.4	13.3

*Crop farming units, comprising approx. 500 farms.
Compiled from Peter Michael Schmitz and Stephan Wiegand, *Die Zukünftige Entwicklung der Landwirtschaft in den fünf neuen Bundesländern*, Kiel, 1991, and EC Commission Report, *The Position of Agriculture in the Community*, Brussels/Luxembourg, 1991, T/20.

Workforce
Some 10% of the workforce of the former GDR were employed in the agricultural sector, as compared with 5% in the Federal Republic and only 2% in the UK. As much as 60% of the workforce were directly involved in production (an average of 8.2 workers per 100 hectares), exceeding west German levels (6.8 per 100 hectares). Even having taken into account statutory employment conditions, such overmanning was unjustifiable. The high labour/land ratio was a basic weakness and the main cause of substantial productivity shortfalls. Other possible explanations

for low productivity levels included the lack of appropriate technology and low levels of automation, which in turn required far more manual labour; frequent breakdowns of machinery which resulted in interrupted working patterns; inadequate adjustment between available work and hours worked because of statutory working hours and holidays; compulsory employment; lack of motivation amongst the workforce; and a high rate of absenteeism through sickness.

The restructuring process means that almost 50% of the sector's workforce will be superfluous. According to official estimates, only 400,000 workers will be required after restructuring.[1] Forty per cent of the excess labour supply is made up of the 'support network', including those employed in 'cultural and social activities' (building work, repairs, crèches, holiday homes, etc.). In addition to the huge social problems envisaged as a result of the mass shedding of labour, the high level of specialization among the 'productive' workforce and a lack of 'all-rounders' who can take on the role of farmers rather than workers in a collective are major obstacles to those wishing to take advantage of government-assisted schemes to restructure the large cooperatives into family-sized holdings (a process known as the *Wiedereinrichtung*).

Prices
Since the last GDR agricultural price reform in 1984 producer prices had risen by 52%, putting agricultural sector incomes on a par with those employed elsewhere in the economy. This system of high producer prices was aimed at stimulating production in the drive towards self-sufficiency.[2] The opening of the border between east and west revealed considerable price distortions in GDR agricultural produce. Based on real exchange-rate values, the prices were some 60–80% of the west German CAP-based equivalent; farm product prices were set at average production-cost-covering levels which guaranteed a certain profit margin. Low and stable consumer prices for basic foodstuffs were guaranteed via state subsidies, even though the quality and availability fluctuated. This subsidization accounted for 15% of state expenditure, and was thus a great burden on the GDR budget. It also encouraged high consumption and the wasteful use of food destined for human consumption as animal feed, e.g. bread, rolled oats, milk products and potatoes.

The gap between production costs and consumer prices meant that most LPGs were uncompetitive once exposed to a west European price regime. The EC price regime had come under downward pressure due to growing surpluses and mounting external pressure for CAP reform via the GATT Uruguay Round. The combination of falling prices and a change in the pattern of consumer preferences after unification led to the almost total collapse of the GDR's internal agricultural produce market.

The agricultural processing industry

The food processing industry, employing some 240,000 workers, was organized into *Kombinate* on a product-by-product basis. Since 1981 investment had shown a negative rate of growth, resulting in obsolescent machinery, inferior produce and a poor general performance. The food processing industry was even less competitive than primary agricultural production. This has proved to be another major obstacle to development, reflected in sales and marketing difficulties immediately after GEMSU.[3]

Trade

The principle of agricultural self-sufficiency involved minimizing imports of foodstuffs. Imports were mainly from the countries of the CMEA, which was the GDR's largest trading partner, and thus east German consumers were deprived of traditional Mediterranean exports, such as citrus fruits, vegetables and wine. Around 10% of agricultural produce and foodstuffs was exported to west Germany under a special arrangement with the EC, which was terminated in 1990. Exports covered by the agreement were animals for slaughter and meat products, i.e. mostly raw products, which were then processed further in the Federal Republic.

The integration of the sector into the Federal Republic and the CAP

Basic legal framework

Immediately upon unification the entire legal framework of the FRG was extended to the new Bundesländer. This included the CAP price support mechanism, quotas and structural funds, as well as EC export subsidies and the refund and levy systems relating to external trade. The GDR also agreed to adapt its production and environmental protection measures to the CAP, including the set-aside of land and afforestation.

In order to facilitate the adjustment process, provisions were made for the progressive application of certain regulatory measures. Some regulations which had been introduced in the GDR remained in force, notably the LPG law and the law on the transfer of property rights and leaseholds of state-owned property and enterprises, members of cooperatives and others. The Agricultural Adjustment Law (*Landwirtschaftsanpassungs-gesetz*, LAG) outlined the legal basis for restoration and guarantee of private ownership of property and for the development of a diverse agricultural sector. It also regulated the process of breaking up the cooperative cartels, which were to be restructured into different legal companies; transferring farms to private ownership (with the aim of reviving family-sized farming units); and implementing regulatory measures, necessary for the planned restructuring. The LAG was intended to clarify disputed property claims and facilitate land reform, in order to speed up the creation of a competitive agricultural sector. However, the law was rushed through the Volkskammer under tremendous pressure of time, and further legislation was soon necessary to deal with many originally unforeseen problems.

Integration into the single European market
Since unification, there has been a fundamental change in the framework within which agriculture in the new Bundesländer has had to operate. The restructuring process, aimed at achieving long-term competitiveness within the single European market, has had to take place against the background of discussions on CAP reforms and agricultural subsidies, as well as the wider GATT negotiations, which have complicated any adaptation measures.

Improved access to inputs (such as investment and agricultural technology) and new incentives under CAP should have raised output. Initially, however, this was not possible because of bottlenecks in the food processing industry, which required urgent government investment to avoid bankruptcies on a massive scale. The structure of agricultural enterprises is to be revolutionized: crop and livestock production units are to be combined, non-agricultural production phased out and the utilized agricultural land per unit reduced, because whole rural communities were built up round the local LPGs. The massive redundancy created by this restructuring risks creating social problems on a huge scale. Such structural adjustments will inevitably demand additional Community expenditure from the structural funds, including the European Agricultural Guidance and Guarantee Fund (EAGGF). This will in turn affect Germany's willingness to continue to contribute to the Community's farm price and income support system.

As in all sectors of the economy, interim measures to deal with these adjustment problems were necessary for both the GDR and the member states of the Community. The Commission gave assurances that it would pay special attention to developments in the agricultural produce markets. Its proposals were based on the principle of as few derogations as possible; those that were unavoidable were subject to strict time limits, applying until 31 December 1993. The danger was that the ensuing market difficulties could be used by other member states as grounds for continuing domestic protection measures.

As of 1 July 1990 (with the implementation of the *Staatsvertrag*) a complicated grant and quota system for intra-German agricultural trade was applied. Its aim was to ease the adjustment process by diminishing and controlling the flow of goods, thus protecting east Germany's food processing industry from bankruptcy, whilst at the same time satisfying the sharply increasing demand for west German products in the east. Effectively the system allowed for west German products to enter the GDR for processing without control, whilst the same privilege did not apply in the opposite direction. At the Commission there was some concern about this intra-German protocol, which had been implemented without prior discussion with Brussels. The procedure was scrutinized to see if it was compatible with the CAP and the completion of the single market. The ensuing outcry by both the east Germans and other member states led to west Germany's request for a full opening of the border. As from 1 August 1990, agricultural products from the GDR could be freely exported to all EC member states, so long as they complied with minimum Community standards on quality and health. Slaughterhouses were notably unable to meet such standards, at least at first.

Production quotas for milk and sugar had to be increased; there was some dispute within the Community over the level of the latter.[4] Adjustments were made to intervention quantities for beef, skimmed milk powder and butter. During 1990/91 beef and pigmeat prices within the EC fell. In the case of beef this was partly caused by overproduction in the GDR. In France there was particular pressure on prices as a result of the rise in the number of cattle sent for slaughter. This was due partly to an extended drought, and partly to the impact on international markets of the mass slaughter of cattle in the GDR in order to reduce milk production. The fall in pigmeat prices was almost entirely due to the enforced slaughter of enormous numbers of sows which were deemed to be in environmentally unacceptable production units. The result was a reduction in the new Länder's pig herds by 50%, which was very damaging to the *Volkseigene Güter*, and meant reduced competition for west German pig farmers. For grain surpluses both private and state storage, as well as transitional intervention measures, were examined.

The restructuring process in the new Bundesländer
In regional, structural and social agricultural policy the adaptation to Community law was far more difficult. The interim measures agreed on 4 December 1990 for improving structural efficiency concentrated on several key points, such as the set-aside of land, the re-establishment and modernization of individual (family) units, the reorganization of the LPGs and compensation for the less-favoured areas. The goal was to make adjustment socially acceptable.

The Commission was sympathetic to state aid awarded to agricultural enterprises and remained neutral as regards the type of organizational and property structure best suited to the region. Existing measures were therefore adjusted to fit the needs of both large cooperative holdings and family farms. Maximum eligible levels for investment aid were increased to allow for this.

The cost of adjustment to CAP price structures was enormous: an estimated increase of DM5.27bn to the GDR budget, rising to DM9.1bn for 1991. This included allowances for set-aside, for clearing apple plantations, for reducing milk production and the price of diesel fuel, and for introducing environmentally friendly farming techniques. The greater part of the funds allocated for 1990, some DM2.2bn, was used for adjustment and bridging loans. Expenditure on product regulation accounted for DM1.5bn, general agricultural funds DM625m and expenditure on structural improvements DM302m.

The most serious adjustment problems for agriculture in the new Bundesländer were the structural difficulties, profit levels, workers' productivity, alignment of production and marketing quality, and environmental standards. In this regard the LPGs fared especially badly. Many cooperatives soon found themselves in severe financial difficulties through falling sales: only a third of the 4,000 LPGs were expected to survive GEMSU without difficulty (thanks to favourable currency conversion terms); a further third required interim assistance from the banks; and the rest would have collapsed but for liquidity credits backed by the government. The GDR Ministerial Council decided to implement an immediate assistance programme, which for July 1990 alone amounted to an additional DM300m, and in August DM400m, to keep firms afloat. The total liquidity requirement for the agricultural sector amounted to DM1.3bn for July. This was far in excess of budgetary targets, but was considered unavoidable to protect the coming harvest.

Breaking up the old structures and adapting to the new system was an extraordinarily difficult task and there was a lot of confusion. The Federal

Agriculture Ministry was accused of failing to understand the problem and of seeking to further the interests of west German farmers. The structure of west German farms was based on more small, potentially less competitive units, but from Bonn's point of view agricultural enterprises run on industrial lines had no future and it thus favoured a revival of family farming units. Bonn's hoped-for '*Wiedereinrichtung* boom' has, however, yet to materialize.

There are several possible reasons for the poor take-up of government incentives to assist in setting up family farms. First, there was continued uncertainty over property ownership. The former LPG law remained valid until 31 December 1991, thus delaying the start of the restructuring process, since farmers owned only 5–20% of the land, inventory and capital of the cooperative and could easily be outvoted on any decision to break it up. Amendments to the LAG clarified the legal position of the members of cooperatives and improved the conditions for opting out, with pay-outs to be set against the budget for former GDR debts.

Second, land is leased by the Treuhand only on a short-term basis, given the legal uncertainties over the compatibility of the proposed land reforms with the *Grundgesetz*. Some improvements resulted from the introduction of a law allowing the Treuhand to lease land for up to twelve years, under certain conditions.

Third, an enormous sum of capital is required to modernize existing plant and machinery. The capital requirement per reconstructed family unit is estimated at around DM700,000, which is way above the ceiling on investment assistance. Many older farmers in particular were also dissuaded by the high level and high risks of borrowing required. Given the average LPG unit of around 30 hectares, a further 100–200 hectares needs to be rented in order to make a business viable, either from LPG members not in the cooperative or from the Treuhand. So far the Treuhand has only offered such rentals on a one-year lease. This means individual farmers have too little collateral to secure adequate bank credit financing. The situation is slowly changing but there is also a genuine desire among many ex-LPG members to share the risks of farming either in a reformed cooperative or through a farming company. Such a model is at odds with the traditional west German practice.

Fourth, because of the previous system most agricultural workers are specialists and thus lack the all-round experience needed to manage such a farming unit. Thus most farmers have chosen to remain within the cooperatives or state holdings, as revised under common law, and to work together, which of course spreads the risk.

Despite all these obstacles, there are attractions in such a structure for potential west German or other investors, whether private farmers or agri-industrialists. For example, the east has many large estates (500–1,000 hectares) available for leasing, especially in the former border regions, which simply do not exist in the west, or only at high leasing charges.

What is particularly disturbing in the east is the lack of time available for farmers to adapt to changing relationships and, more importantly, to put together the necessary capital. East German farming officials had assumed that the federal government would take this into account. The last Agricultural Law to be passed by the Volkskammer had given local residents the right of pre-emption and pre-leasing, but this was later repealed as part of the negotiations on the unification treaty as the result of pressure by the west German farmers' lobby.

Such an agricultural policy set in motion a development which west Germany had hoped to avoid: after the restructuring there will be many large farming units which will be worked either by large west German owners or by successors to the LPGs.

Effects of CAP reforms

An agreement on CAP reforms was finally reached on 22 May 1992, six months after Commissioner Ray MacSharry's initial proposals were put forward. The central pillar of the reforms is a 29% reduction in cereal prices over three years with *full* compensation to farmers for market revenue losses due to a fall in market price supports. Moreover, 15% of arable land is to be put into set-aside. This has helped UK farmers somewhat, since otherwise their units, which are typically larger than the EC average, would have suffered extremely badly. In this respect, the German agricultural minister, Ignaz Kiechle, was happy to support British demands for compensation to be paid to both big and small farms, given that the model emerging in the new Bundesländer also needed to be taken into account. The compensation payments will be based on average past yields; this will disadvantage eastern Germany, where the calculation is not directly comparable with that in other member states.

Large units and medium-sized units with significant income subsidies would have to reckon with substantial income losses which could not be compensated for by increased production or falling production costs. The impact of the reforms on the (west) German model will very likely mean a restructuring process that lowers overheads – in other words, a move towards agricultural industrialization. This is not the 'preferred' model for the restructuring process in the former GDR. Nevertheless it is the large farm, rather than the family farm so prevalent in Western Europe over the past forty years, which is capable of competing with minimal support on the world market.

The cuts in cereal prices are supposed also to bring about a fall in the cost of animal feeds to support a 15% cut in beef price supports and a 5% cut in the price of butter. Production quotas are to be applied also to sheepmeat and beef. A reduction of prices will improve the consumer's position only if the price decreases are actually passed on in full to the consumer. What is agreed by all is that the changes in agricultural policy will result in an increase in the EAGGF and thus there has to be a wide consensus on the outcome.

Summary, prospects and effect on EC

The integration of the former GDR into the Federal Republic meant that Germany had to integrate a totally different agricultural structure not only into its social market economy but also into the CAP.

The application of the CAP was relatively unproblematic. Much more difficult was the actual restructuring of the sector. The continuing un-certainty over property rights and legal rights, together with the shortage of adequate capital or an appropriate training profile, make farmers reluctant to take on units at their own risk, especially when uncertainty over CAP reforms and the outcome of the Uruguay Round (both of which will have a considerable impact on the future of east German farmers) is taken into account.

The entry of the GDR into the CAP meant a worsening of agricultural market difficulties in the EC, especially in terms of potential increases in surplus production and also increased exports as subsidies were removed. This demanded extra structural payments, export subsidies and the added budgetary burden of intervention purchases, which has made the German government stronger in its resistance to its farm lobby and less willing to contribute to Community farm price and income support.

Primary interest in investment in the new Länder has been from (west) Germans especially in basic agricultural products and food processing industries. Foreign interest came primarily from the Netherlands and Denmark, not only because of their proximity but also because of the size of the farming units. West German farmers also have welcomed the opportunity to lease or buy a much larger unit. British firms have shown an interest in investing in the region but suffer from both language difficulties and unfamiliarity with the local market. From the British point of view the land there is quite poor and not suitable for crop farming. British companies are more likely to become involved in an advisory capacity, given their long experience in effective management and the modern production methods suited to larger farming units.

British farmers had expressed considerable concern over the MacSharry reform proposals. The integration of the former GDR, with its large-scale units, into the EC and CAP drew Britain and Germany closer together, as Britain hoped for a softening of the German position on CAP reforms. Although in west Germany the view was that units in the east were too large, west German agriculture, with its small farms, remains uncompetitive within the EC relative to average incomes. The trend in west Germany has thus been increasingly towards larger units. The structure which will evolve will reflect models of both east and west. Whilst in the west larger units are pursued for economic reasons, in the new Länder the aim is to achieve flexibility and efficiency, while also attempting to protect the environment; thus unit size will adjust downwards. In the long run it is estimated the average unit size in eastern Germany will be between 200 and 1,000 hectares. Such units will have a good chance of becoming competitive within the EC, and indeed on the world market.

Within those EC member states where agriculture is not organized around predominantly small farmers and is competitive (e.g. Britain, the Netherlands and Denmark), hopes that the GATT framework for liberalization and CAP reforms would change Germany's position have been partly realized in spite of domestic pressure. Thus the impact of unification on the Community in this sector has been considerable, with important implications for the future pattern of world trade.

9

CASE-STUDY: SHIPBUILDING

Structural problems are endemic in the EC shipbuilding industry. Ever since the late 1970s merchant shipbuilders have been undergoing a painful process of restructuring: capacity has been reduced by 53% in the Community as a whole and by as much as 75% in the UK. The ability to compete on world markets would not have been possible in the past without regular Community subsidies and the sector is one in which degressive national assistance is accepted, agreed annually by the EC. At the time of German unification the 6th Directive on aid to shipbuilding applied. The Commission took the view that the provisions of that directive, as well as those included within the draft of the 7th Directive, could be applied without modification to east Germany so far as restructuring aid was concerned. However, it also recognized that a higher level of operating aid than applied in other Community yards would be necessary. These special arrangements were to be included in the negotiations for an international agreement concerning aid to shipbuilding, under examination within the OECD.[1] The Council, the Commission and the German government were urged to table proposals[2] to this effect, which were not debated in the European Parliament until July 1992.[3]

The east German shipbuilding industry

The shipbuilding industry in the former GDR had been reconstructed after 1945 as part of the country's war reparations to the Soviet Union, with exports to that country accounting for 80% of the total. The industry was badly equipped, seriously overmanned and grossly inefficient, using highly uncompetitive methods of assembly. As in other industrial sectors in the GDR, the introduction of GEMSU exacerbated these difficulties and meant that not one of the contracts signed before July 1990 was profitable – in fact in about thirty per cent of cases the sale price did not even cover the costs of materials. It was feared that the restructuring process, necessary to achieve a level of competitiveness on a par with the rest of the EC shipbuilding industry, would lead to severe social problems. Many of the shipyards were situated in the coastal regions of Mecklenburg–West Pomerania, and were tied to mechanical engineering and directly related service industries in a region where the only alternative employment was agriculture (also badly hit by unification). There were few new contracts signed after GEMSU. The USSR was unable to pay for fifteen of the vessels that were built for it during 1991 once the final prices had been converted into hard currency, despite both federal government credits and Hermes export guarantees.[4] The estimated costs to the taxpayer of berthing, maintenance and insurance of those vessels was put at around DM225,000 per day.[5]

Initial restructuring of the east German shipyards

As part of its earlier activities under the GDR administration, the shipyards as well as their suppliers were merged in June 1990 to form Deutsche Maschinen und Schiffbau AG (DMS). After unification, there were attempts at an extensive restructuring of the industry. Following talks with specialist consultants, DMS submitted a plan to the Treuhand in February 1991, which was refined and accepted in September. The objectives of the plan included the amalgamation of two of the yards (Neptun and Warnow),[6] a move away from traditional shipbuilding in favour of specialist vessels, a reorganization of the production programme in accordance with EC guidelines (a subsidy ceiling of 13% in 1991, falling to 9% in 1992), a restructuring and privatization programme, and substantial reductions in the workforce by the end of 1992 (with a loss of around two-thirds of total employment). The initial fall in jobs was rapid, from 45,000 at the time of unification to 20,000 by 31 December 1991, with the ultimate target of 15,500 by the end of 1995. The whole package, underwritten by the Treuhand, was designed to enable cost-covering contracts to be signed, taking account of competitive capacity and the wage differential between eastern and western German workers, which was expected to disappear by the end of 1994. Bank credits in support of the yards were scheduled to expire in

March 1992. This corresponded to the Treuhand's wishes that the real estate value of DMS should not be undermined by high levels of debt accumulated when it was part of the GDR.

In November 1991 the German government applied to the Commission for approval of shipbuilding subsidies based on EC maximum aid ceilings. The Commission would not grant that approval since it doubted whether the east German yards could keep within the limits.[7] The Commission favoured a new derogation on the 7th Directive,[8] provided the German government presented them with a more radical restructuring concept involving substantial reductions in capacity. The German government continued to resist integrated EC assistance, fearing grave social difficulties should capacity be cut further.

The crisis in the yards at the beginning of 1992

After due consideration a package of measures was presented to the Commission which included a 40% reduction in merchant shipbuilding capacity in the eastern shipyards.[9] In return, production aid was to be granted to a maximum level of 36% of turnover, government servicing of the debts was not to be regarded as state aid and finally the yards were to be privatized. The formula which was eventually accepted in June 1992 by EC Industry Ministers has since proved to be most contentious. The European Parliament, in particular, complained that the decision to proceed had been taken without either itself or the EC Shipbuilders Association being consulted.[10] The general view was that the figures on which the Council had based its decision were fundamentally flawed[11] and that capacity figures had been miscalculated. Further, the proposed reduction in capacity was questioned and it was believed that a 55% reduction would have been more appropriate.

Once they were put out to tender, several buyers were interested in the yards, including the Norwegian Kvaerner group (which wanted the Neptun–Warnow yard). The bid by Kvaerner, a multinational ship-builder, caused much concern in the UK shipbuilding industry that work would be switched from the Govan yard in Scotland to east Germany in order to take advantage of the higher level of subsidy. The workers in the shipyards themselves were unhappy about the prospect of further job losses, which they felt would be all the higher under foreign ownership. They believed they had been badly let down by the Treuhand, and a series of sit-ins took place.

At the beginning of March 1992 the Treuhand decided to sell the

Neptun–Warnow yard to the Kvaerner group. The Meerestechnik yard in Wismar (MTW) and the Dieselmotorenwerk in Rostock were sold together, to the west German firm Bremen Vulkan AG. This decision apparently convinced the Commission that the restructuring of the yards would be complete by the end of 1993 and that the yards could realistically become competitive. This led it to allow yards under private ownership to maintain their entitlement to state subsidies at a level over and above the 9% which applied elsewhere. The decision was subject to approval by the Council of Ministers. However, the Commission's apparent over-anxiousness to react urgently to the crisis in the east German yards meant that it did not seek agreement from the European Parliament. This contravened the whole spirit of the German unification process within the context of European integration, whereby the Parliament was to be consulted on all transitional measures and derogations as well as on other adjustments to secondary Community legislation.[12]

Impact of the provisions on the competitiveness of other EC shipyards

Even before the derogation on production aid and capacity cuts was agreed, the level of assistance to the east German yards had been very high by European standards. Some DM3bn will have been spent on aid to improve the environment, clear former debts and cover the costs of investment and closures up to the end of 1993. When this is added to the estimated value of production aid, the total cost of maintaining some 5,000 jobs comes to DM4.16bn. The new buyers will presumably be able to take advantage of having modernized the yards without needing to cover any debts. This means they will secure earlier returns on their investments, which will give them a distinct competitive advantage over other EC yards.

At a time when shipyards are under pressure from non-EC yards, and world prices are falling, the rise in state aid is believed to have raised prices throughout the Community, with a disastrous impact on EC yards: the Danish shipyards are in crisis; France has paid a heavy price for its restructuring, having reduced capacity by 79%; and in the UK the closure of the Cammell Laird shipyard scheduled for 1993 was believed to be due partly to the absence of a 'level playing-field' in a market distorted by the EC decision on east German yards.[13]

Furthermore, although the derogation is supposed to apply only until the end of 1994 there is considerable doubt as to whether, given the current world crisis, the yards can achieve economic viability. It is also doubtful whether the transparency of the state assistance can be assured and to what extent the Commission can introduce safeguards into the monitoring procedures, since the aid will be in the hands of companies controlled by west German or other European companies.

The British view is that the decision will certainly export unemployment from east Germany to elsewhere in the Community, if it has not already done so.[14] Parallels have been drawn with the case of the modern Sunderland yards which were forced to close in 1988: even though they had a buyer who was prepared to operate without a subsidy, this was not allowed.

Conclusions

Whilst considerable sympathy has been expressed for the plight of the workers in the east German shipyards, the manner in which the question of assistance has been handled has proved to be contentious, not least because the proposal was drawn up by the Commission without consulting key players in either the industry or the European Parliament. The opposition is not over the derogation in itself but in the way in which it has been set up. It is widely believed that this has given rise to unfair conditions of competition. If this is the case, then it is a clear example of an adverse impact of unification on the completion of the internal market. At worst this could undo the very painful efforts throughout the EC to work towards abolition of all state aid for shipbuilding in order to compete more effectively on world markets. In this respect, appeals by the Commission for social solidarity among member states may well wear thin and threaten prospects for consensus on the issue.

10

EXTERNAL IMPLICATIONS

The external aspects of German unification were dealt with in the first instance by modifying the status quo and not by radical change. To all intents and purposes there was no change to either the FRG's external policies or the Community's *acquis communautaire et politique* as regards both common foreign policy stands and common foreign trade. In reality, however, unification clearly began to have an impact on what Germany and its partners thought on a range of foreign policy issues as early as 1990. It became more obvious during 1991 in the light of Germany's response to the Gulf war and its greater assertiveness as displayed over the issue of recognizing Croatia.

Originally it was thought that unification would have generally positive effects on the Community's external policy: first, by enhancing the EC's role as the stable core of a new, unifying Europe eventually encompassing the central and east European countries; and, second, by providing an incentive for internal reforms (ultimately agreed at Maastricht) that would strengthen the Community's role in the world by replacing European Political Cooperation with a Common Foreign and Security Policy (CFSP).[1] These aspirations and expectations found expression in the European Council's Strasbourg declaration: 'At this time of profound and rapid change, the Community is and must remain a point of reference and influence. It remains the cornerstone of a new European architecture and, in its will to openness, a mooring for future European equilibrium.'[2] There were similar expectations about Germany itself.

This chapter considers the implications of unification for Germany's *Osteuropapolitik*, both economically and politically, and for the EC, in the IGC debate on political union and a CFSP.

The Osteuropapolitik of the unified Germany

In the bipolar international system of the postwar era, the political and economic border between east and west coincided with the division of Germany. After unification, Germany's eastern border became the frontier between affluence and relative poverty, between the stability of the EC and the relative instability of countries undergoing radical political and economic reform. This has added a political centrality to Germany's geographical position at the heart of Europe.[3] On the one hand, Germany's role as a cultural, historical and economic bridge between east and west has been, or is being, reconstructed. This places upon Germany an increasing responsibility for handling relations with the eastern and central European states, a responsibility it seeks to fulfil by pursuing an active *Osteuropapolitik* of cooperation, association and integration with these countries within national, European and transatlantic frameworks. On the other hand, Germany's frontier position places it closer than its EC partners to the potential sources of instability in central and eastern Europe which may emerge from the economic and security vacuum left by the collapse of the Warsaw Pact and the CMEA. The federal government in Bonn also feels pressure from its immediate neighbours in central and eastern Europe as well as from Russia and the other CIS states, all of which have high expectations of Germany's ability to help pave the way to EC membership and form a new European order. Most significant in the latter respect is the unspoken political obligation to Moscow because of the largely unconditional Soviet willingness to accept German unification.

For decades Germany has, largely implicitly, assumed the role of seeking to moderate the costs of division: the division of Germany, the division of Europe and the ideological division between East and West. The immediate need in a divided Germany was to help those who had been separated from family and friends. But the need to moderate the effects of the East–West division was equally compelling in a political and security sense, given Germany's front-line position and the dangers of singularization. The FRG therefore promoted cooperation and conflict containment through the EC and other multilateral fora. Since unification this role has been transformed: Germany has used these fora to promote a greater awareness of central European interests and concerns and their effects on Western Europe, particularly the 'spillover risks' of east–west migration. Germany has also promoted the idea of a 'comprehensive security policy' within a Euro-Atlantic Community.[4] Some sections of opinion fear that Germany's interests in the east will irritate its western neighbours and have, somewhat unconvincingly, argued the case for unreserved solidarity with the EC and NATO and against a bridging or central role: *'Nicht Brücke, nicht Mitte'*.[5]

Trade and commercial aspects

The collapse of former GDR/CMEA trade and counter measures
The European Commission at first expected the new Bundesländer to develop a pivotal role in what would become a flourishing external trade with eastern Europe. The GDR's trade links and obligations there were to act as a catalyst for EC trade agreements with the former CMEA countries and thus wider European economic cooperation.[6] But the difficulties of economic adaptation in east Germany, as well as the even more chaotic conditions in the former CMEA states, had a virtually catastrophic effect on trade. More than two years after the *Staatsvertrag* the export sector remains a fundamental weak spot in the development of the new Länder.

These adaptation problems led the EC and the Bonn government to provide transitional assistance measures. From 3 October 1990 to 31 December 1992 (with a possible extension) the EC granted to the six former CMEA countries and Yugoslavia permission to export at zero tariff into the new Bundesländer, provided that the goods originating from these countries were covered by previous purchasing commitments (*Vertrauensschutz*).[7] The EC also lifted current anti-dumping duties and granted exceptions for goods not conforming to EC standards. These measures may have helped a little but were unable to reverse the decline in trade. The former CMEA countries utilized very little of the total possible tariff-free trade into the new Bundesländer – 13% in 1990 and only 7% in 1991.[8]

Faced with a continuing breakdown in these existing trade flows, the FRG government was obliged to take emergency measures. Although east German exports actually showed a slight increase during 1990 while imports from the former CMEA fell by nearly 50%, by mid-1991 imports had dropped to 25% of 1989 levels, and exports from east Germany were only 37% of 1989 levels (see Tables 10.1 and 10.2). The collapse in imports from the six former CMEA countries for 1990 clearly shows that the *Vertrauensschutz* rules were having little effect in safeguarding trade.[9]

External implications

Table 10.1 German imports from Central and Eastern Europe

Country	New Bundesländer			Old Bundesländer		
	1989	1990	1991	1989	1990	1991 (Nov.)
	%			%		
SU/CIS	57.4	61.5	72.2	44.1	41.9	37.6
Poland	11.4	12.2	11.5	18.9	23.7	24.7
Czech.	12.1	11.6	10.7	13.1	12.4	16.3
Hungary	9.1	8.3	3.8	14.1	15.0	15.2
Romania	5.0	2.7	1.2	8.1	5.1	4.3
Bulgaria	4.9	3.7	0.6	1.7	1.8	1.9
Total	DM millions			DM millions		
	26,793	14,812	6,239	19,012	21,756	24,008
Country	Change on previous year (%)					
SU/CIS		-40.8	-47.3		8.7	9.0
Poland		-41.2	-58.2		44.1	27.6
Czech.		-47.0	-59.7		8.5	59.7
Hungary		-49.4	-79.5		21.6	24.1
Romania		-69.5	-80.7		-27.5	1.1
Bulgaria		-58.8	-93.5		21.1	27.4
EC/Europe		-44.7	-55.5		14.4	21.9

Source: Statistisches Bundesamt Wiesbaden, Fachserie 7, Reihe 1, December 1990, June 1991, November 1991.

New opportunities

Although exports from the eastern and central European countries into the new Bundesländer fell dramatically after GEMSU, this was not the case for Germany as a whole. In 1991 the countries which now have association agreements with the EC, namely Hungary, Poland and the then Czech and Slovak Federal Republic (CFSR), were able to increase their exports to Germany considerably. For the six European CMEA countries Germany continued to be the largest western trade partner. For Poland, Hungary and the CSFR, Germany is now the largest trading

110

Table 10.2 German exports to Central and Eastern Europe

	New Bundesländer			Old Bundesländer		
	1989	1990	1991	1989	1990	1991 (Nov.)
Country	%			%		
SU/CIS	57.4	59.8	79.0	47.2	44.3	33.6
Poland	10.8	9.9	8.9	18.3	20.0	28.6
Czech.	13.2	11.5	5.7	11.2	13.2	16.3
Hungary	9.0	9.1	3.3	14.9	14.4	15.1
Romania	4.9	5.1	2.0	2.4	4.8	3.8
Bulgaria	4.7	4.8	1.2	6.0	3.4	2.6
Total	DM millions			DM millions		
	28,893	29,723	10,686	24,438	23,394	23,248
Country	Change on previous year (%)					
SU/CIS		7.1	-46.7		-10.2	-19.7
Poland		-5.5	-62.4		4.9	62.4
Czech.		-10.7	-80.8		12.7	40.5
Hungary		3.8	-85.5		-7.8	14.0
Romania		5.3	-84.5		90.8	-12.6
Bulgaria		3.7	-90.7		-46.4	-19.0
EC/Europe		2.9	-59.9		-4.3	8.8

Source: Statistisches Bundesamt Wiesbaden, Fachserie 7, Reihe 1, December 1990, June 1991, November 1991.

partner of all. The GDR had been heavily dependent on the USSR for exports, and even today the CIS is the new Bundesländer's most important partner in the east (1991 import share: 71.41%). Compared with the rest of the EC the new Bundesländer's trade structure was naturally heavily skewed towards the east. The former CMEA's share in total imports fell to just under 60% (in 1990) and exports were about 78% of total GDR/new Bundesländer imports. This compared with about 3% for the EC as a whole, or 4% for the old FRG, for both imports and exports from the former CMEA. Eastern export markets still account for

Table 10.3 Comparison of German and EC trade with Eastern Europe

	1989	1990	1991 (1st ¹/₂yr)	1991 (Nov.)
			Imports	
New Bundesländer (bn DM)	26.8	14.8	3.7	6.2
Old Bundesländer (bn DM)	19.0	21.8	12.4	24.0
EC (bn ecus)	27.2	30.0	17.0	—
			Percentage of total imports	
New Bundesländer	65.2	64.8	62.9	58.5
Old Bundesländer	3.8	3.9	3.9	4.1
EC	2.5	2.7	2.8	—
			Exports	
New Bundesländer (bn DM)	28.9	29.7	5.5	10.7
Old Bundesländer (bn DM)	24.4	23.4	12.3	23.2
EC (bn ecus)	24.1	27.1	15.0	—
			Percentage of total exports	
New Bundesländer	70.3	78.1	65.1	65.6
Old Bundesländer	3.8	3.6	3.8	3.9
EC	2.3	2.5	2.7	—

Source: Statistisches Bundesamt Wiesbaden; Institut für Angewandte Wirt-schaftsforschung, *Der Außenhandel der neuen deutschen Bundesländer mit Mittel- und Osteuropa – Chancen und Risiken*, Berlin, 1991.

the bulk of the new Bundesländer's foreign trade.[10] Poland, Hungary and the CSFR have also been able to compete against the traditionally privileged position of USSR trade by a greater product diversification, but to date only in the FRG market, not yet in the EC as a whole.[11]

As Table 10.3 shows, Germany continues to dominate trade between the OECD/EC and the central and east European economies. At the end of 1989 one-third of eastern trade with all OECD countries was with the FRG. Germany's share of total EC eastern trade in 1990 was 37.8% for imports and 56.7% of exports. It is followed at a substantial distance by Italy, France comes third, and Britain's share of EC total imports and exports was 8.2% and 6.2% respectively. From January to November 1991 the united Germany was able to increase its share to 45.5% of imports and 57.8% of exports, compared with a fall in Britain's share to 6.3% and 4.6% respectively. Therefore although the benefits at the moment are pretty meagre because of the setbacks in the new Bundesländer's trade with the east, the unified Germany seems likely to profit more than the old FRG from the opening of markets and the completion of free trade zones between the EC and Poland, Hungary and the CSFR. For the EC as a whole eastern Europe will remain of interest as a possible area of trade growth after the completion of the EC's internal market.

Germany took measures to avoid the total collapse of eastern trade, largely because of the effects on employment in the new Bundesländer.[12] In December 1990 Hermes export credit guarantees were introduced for trade with the USSR for 1991 and risk coverage for credit was raised from 85% to 100%.[13] With 280 (DM9,689m) out of 329 (DM9,858m) valid contracts, the former USSR was the front-runner in Hermes credits taken up by exporters in the new Bundesländer. It was followed by the CFSR and Romania with nine valid contracts, Poland three, Yugoslavia two and Hungary one.[14] In spite of preferential treatment for east German firms (shipbuilding, machine assembly), the west German firms which were heavily committed to eastern markets were able to maintain their position.

Finally there is the question of the compatibility of export credits to sustain east German trade with EC or OECD rules. The employment issue figures largely in the case for subsidies because there are still some 600,000 jobs directly or indirectly dependent on trade with central and eastern Europe. Criticisms of the restructuring process and a 'Hermes mentality' are as frequent as calls for a new system of sector-specific export credits within the framework of a controlled industrial policy. A move towards sector-specific export regimes could, however, provoke a conflict with the EC Commission, which has for some time avoided making an issue of its doubts about the compatibility of Hermes credits with the EC rules on subsidies.

Prospects

If the external trade balance of the new Bundesländer is to recover over the longer term, it is vital for them to develop a product mix which is attractive to both EC and OECD markets. Exports from these Länder to central and eastern Europe are mostly mechanical engineering products, vehicles, finished products and manufactured goods. There have been significant increases in the export share for food products, including meat and milk products. This contrasts with a fall in mechanical engineering and chemicals exports, both sectors which had previously made a major contribution to the GDR's external trade.

Any competitive advantages of the five new Länder in eastern trade, such as established delivery and distribution networks, knowledge of the markets or geographical proximity, are limited and disappearing rapidly. The expectation that they would become a 'gateway to the east', and thereby an attractive location for both German and foreign investors, has proved to be too optimistic. As Chapter 5 has shown, this was largely due to the rapid rise in wage costs, but also to the relative poverty of infrastructure and, in the early stages of unification, uncertainties about economic progress. Investment is also attracted away from the new Bundesländer and towards other countries such as Hungary or the CSFR, where wage costs have remained lower than in the EC.

Given the enormous difficulties facing the central and east European economies, German firms are likely to pay greater attention to the EFTA markets now that these countries are seeking EC membership. Furthermore exports, primarily to the EC and other OECD countries, account for 35–40% of the FRG's gross domestic product. Maintaining open access to these markets therefore remains Germany's overriding interest.

The German government has increasingly complained of being pushed beyond the limits of its financial capabilities in its support for the central and east European states, which has has totalled DM90bn since 1989. Bonn is now urging its partners to carry their fair share of the burden, arguing that Germany is providing 'well over half of all western aid to the CIS and almost a third of all western aid to the countries in central, eastern and southern Europe'.[15] For the PHARE aid programme alone Germany is the biggest single donor, providing some 32.21% of funds, compared with 32.4% via the EC and less than 1% from Britain.[16]

Political aspects

German and EC treaties with central and eastern Europe
German foreign policy includes the concept of *Westbindung plus Ostverbindungen* (ties to the west with links to the east).[17] Even as unification was being negotiated, the FRG was preparing for a second generation of treaties with its eastern neighbours. Just as the Moscow treaty with the USSR in 1970 was followed by a series of treaties with the central and east European countries, the so-called 'Grand Treaty' of 1991 with the

USSR was followed by agreements with Poland (June 1991), Bulgaria (October 1991), Hungary and the CSFR (both in February 1992), and Romania in March 1992. These agreements were oriented towards the new (post-cold war) Europe. France and Italy subsequently concluded similar bilateral agreements, but Britain has been less active and systematic, preferring multilateral association agreements.

Germany's bilateral treaties with the eastern countries seek to send political signals of good-neighbourliness, replacing the treaties of the 1970s; they are also influenced by the legacies of national socialism and the Second World War. They do, however, refer to multilateral treaties such as the CSCE (over treatment of minorities and peaceful resolution of disputes). Finally they express German support for the integration of these countries in the EC. The EC's receptive position on unification may also have moved the Community, out of fairness or solidarity, to press ahead with the association agreements with the central and east Europeans.

So far the bilaterals have paralleled the EC association agreements. Although the central and east Europeans see Germany as a major partner in the west, it is with Brussels that they must negotiate for enhanced market access. In this respect there is scope for joint efforts by Britain and Germany in pressing for improvements in the EC position.

The impact on CFSP

Germany and France called early on for the inclusion of a common foreign and security policy within European political union (EPU), in their joint statement in April 1990. The fact that German and French interests merged in favour of integration in this key area of national sovereignty was in no small part due to German unification.[18] West Germany had long expressed a willingness, indeed a desire, for some form of CFSP (as expressed, for example, in the Genscher/Colombo plan of 1981). The FRG also wanted to use the 'window of opportunity' offered by the upheavals of 1989 and the move towards unification itself to advance such an objective, in order to allay any fears among its neighbours about the foreign policy of a larger unified Germany. Bonn also believed that it was an opportune time to realize its long-held objective of creating a permanent institutional structure within which the Twelve could develop common foreign policies. At no point, however, was there any questioning of Germany's commitment to preserving the political and institutional structures of the transatlantic alliance. The issue was more one of how to strengthen the European voice.

However, when it came to the debate on formal proposals for CFSP within the IGC on political union, the implications of German unification formed part of a 'hidden agenda' behind the explicit Community agenda. Britain, in particular, did not accept the 'window of opportunity' argument. Paris, too, was far from convinced of the advisability of moving towards common foreign policies, and it was, in fact, a Franco-British minority which won the day in Dresden in May 1991 in the debate over whether CFSP should be an integral part of the EC or form a more intergovernmental pillar of European Union. But Britain appeared less concerned than France about a German *Alleingang*, though more doubtful about the wider issue of the desirability and efficacy of a supranational foreign policy for the EC.

It is significant that both in Germany and elsewhere in the EC the issue of Germany's international role and responsibilities after unification only really surfaced during the Gulf war and the Yugoslav crisis, not during the height of the debate on unification. Whenever it began, the fact that the issue has emerged suggests that doubts remain about Germany's reliability and dependability as a partner in any 'security Community'.[19] During the Gulf war Germany demonstrated it was not ready to fulfil any new international role or even act as part of a 'partnership in leadership'. Early in the Yugoslav crisis the then Foreign Minister, Hans-Dietrich Genscher, in pressing for the recognition of Croatia, risked isolating his country within the EC – something Germany has always tried to avoid. The central issue is the interpretation of the *Grundgesetz* on the deployment of the Bundeswehr in out-of-area activities by NATO, as well as Germany's participation in UN peacekeeping or peace-making forces, and an interpretation of Article 5 of the NATO Treaty. There is also the problem of convincing the German population of the compelling need for German military contributions in order to defend the international order.[20] Interim assessments of the responses to the Gulf crisis suggest that within the CFSP the constant shifting between national intergovernmental strategies and common EC activities will be most significant,[21] and that German foreign policy has largely consisted of pragmatic responses to events. The realization of the major policy objectives of national unity and East–West detente left a vacuum in Germany's foreign policy programme which simply could not be filled by lofty statements supporting European federalism and cooperative internationalism.

The debate on CFSP within the Community was influenced by internal and external factors. The two internal factors were, first, the desire of some of Germany's partners, France in particular, to tie Germany to a

Community foreign policy stance and avoid any German *Sonderweg* or German supremacy in external affairs; and, second, the spillover effects on EPC of integration in other areas (e.g. the impact of the Single European Act). External factors included the upheavals in eastern Europe and the growing calls for a Community response to the risk of instability emanating from its eastern frontier; the suspicion of American dis-engagement from Europe, except from anything to do with the USSR/CIS; and the challenges of the Gulf war and the Yugoslav crisis.

These external factors were not always interpreted in the same fashion. For example, France saw a US disengagement as possible and indeed desirable and indeed called for a stronger European defence policy via WEU, whereas for Britain and the Netherlands it required measures to strengthen the Atlantic alliance. During the preparations for the intergovernmental conferences Germany worked closely with France, even though the two countries held quite divergent positions on security and defence matters. Germany was generally in favour of maintaining a balance between a stronger role for the EC in defence, as a means of preventing a renationalization of defence policy in the wake of the collapse of the USSR, and a desire to retain NATO and a US military presence in Europe. Between April 1990 and October 1991 a total of five common initiatives were formulated.[22]

Some government negotiators have criticized the joint Franco-German negotiating positions for being too late and too general, and thus less effective than the representations of individual member states, with a limited impact on the outcome of the IGC debate on CFSP. In almost all of the key CFSP issues the UK took the opposite position. Thus despite the differences between the French and German positions, traditional coalition models within the Community continued throughout the IGC. The British delegation stood by its intergovernmental approach and actively participated in the formulation of the Maastricht CFSP text.[23]

The outcome of Maastricht is broadly interpreted within the EC as the result of an internal dynamic. From Germany's point of view this represents a shift in perception, since it considered the external factors to be the more important motivating force. The international crises of 1990/91 have, if anything, strengthened rather than weakened this view.[24] For Germany and for the more integrationist circles in the EC, the Gulf crisis showed the need for a common policy and even suggested that the option of a qualitative leap towards a full integration of EPC in the EC was a possibility. But for Britain the crisis illustrated the limits of common action and the need for cooperation by means of an intergovernmental approach. Again it should not be forgotten that France shared many of Britain's concerns about bringing foreign and security policy within the Community and favoured retaining control of it within the European Council.

Maastricht fails to match the German 'offer'

The broad message coming from Germany was that it was prepared to cede part of its newly regained (full) sovereignty to the Community in order to allay fears of a dominant Germany. Kohl and Genscher therefore made an ambitious 'offer' to the Community on political union, in parallel with EMU, which was in the end only partially realized in the Treaty on European Union. The sections on CFSP fell short of the German ideas about procedures, coverage and institutional arrangements.

On *procedures* the introduction of qualified majority voting is confined to common foreign and security policy matters and does not apply to defence. The compromise formula on joint action contained in Article J.3(3) further allows each member state the right of veto in every phase of a joint action to delay the passing of a resolution. Unanimity will apply until such time as a (unanimous) decision is taken to provide for qualified majority voting in a particular area of joint action.

On *coverage* Maastricht stops some way short of the menu of possible areas of joint action contained in the original Franco-German proposal. It does refer to CFSP extending to all areas of foreign and security policy, 'including the eventual framing of a common defence policy, which might in time lead to a common defence' (Art. J4(1)). Both the French and German governments see this article as a very positive development. But there is no specific reference in CFSP to a 'European peace order' or a 'new European architecture'. In German eyes the CFSP also fails to reflect either the profound changes now occurring in Europe or the increased responsibility of the Community (or European Union) for maintaining European order (apart from the pledge to protect such normative values as peace and democracy). For many German observers this means there is no binding treaty obligation to work for convergence, and consensus among the Twelve on key questions of foreign policy remains.

Similarly Bonn feels that the protocol on 'joint action' attached to the Maastricht agreement falls short of the Franco-German proposals with regard to both the regional priorities of CFSP (which are not mentioned in the Treaty of Union at all) and the tasks concerning defence policy. The priorities for 'joint action' are given as the new areas of common interest, such as the CSCE process, disarmament, arms control and nuclear

118

non-proliferation. But the protocol list does not include ideas for joint action included in the Franco-German proposal of October 1991, such as political and economic relations with the former Soviet Union; political and economic relations and cooperation with the central and east European countries; relations with the United States and Canada on the basis of a common declaration made in November 1990; political and economic relations with southern and eastern Mediterranean countries; cooperation with the United Nations and other international organizations; and participation in humanitarian assistance measures. Interestingly the Franco-German list contained reference to the need for 'participation in peacekeeping measures especially within the framework of the United Nations'. The precise details of joint action areas and subjects were handed over to the Commission's Report (on CFSP) to the Lisbon European Council of June 1992.

With regard to *institutions*, the Maastricht agreement largely formalized the informal arrangements that had been developed to implement Title III of the Single European Act. If ratified it will mean that meetings of foreign ministers within EPC will be combined with the meetings of the Council for Foreign and Security Policy, as well as confirming the leading role of the European Council in the CFSP. There is also to be a merging of the European Council and EPC secretariats and joint sittings of the COREPER and the Political Committee. The role of the Commission is to be enhanced by granting it the (joint) right of initiative and full participation in work on CFSP. But the European Parliament is to get no additional powers of control or decision-making over and above the modifications to Article 228 (EEC) on agreements between the EC and third countries.

As regards the relationship between WEU, NATO and the European Union, an issue disputed between member states, the Maastricht agreement leans towards a solution favouring a greater role for WEU but without placing it under the European Council, as was suggested in the Franco-German proposal. This proposal contained contradictions which were picked up by member states (including Britain and the Netherlands) concerned about the likely impact on transatlantic relations. The solution found was that the Council is to decide on practical arrangements 'in agreement with the institutions of the WEU'. According to the Maastricht Treaty, WEU is an 'integral part of the development of the Union' (Article J.4(2)). It should elaborate and implement decisions and actions of the Union at the Union's request, and its operational role should be strengthened by having military units attached to it. Article J.4(4) also adds the safeguard, for countries like Britain, that it is for member states to determine how they satisfy their commitments to NATO.

Appraisal

German unification may have been an important factor in the decision to start a second IGC on political union, but the Maastricht text on CFSP suggests that it subsequently had little impact on the substance of the negotiations. The German negotiating stance on EMU would have been little different, with or without unification. On EPU and specifically CFSP, however, Bonn might have felt constrained by virtue of its intra-German policy objectives had unification not happened.[25] France extended its advocacy of anchoring the united Germany within the EC to the debate on CFSP, which was to become both an instrument and a platform of France's new foreign policy. The majority of EC member states, particularly Britain, either were less concerned than France about the possibility of a German *Sonderweg* in foreign policy or considered a substantial shift from intergovernmental to supranational forms of foreign policy cooperation an inappropriate response to the new political conditions in Germany and Europe after unification. Rather than change established views, the international and European crises of 1991 tended to consolidate existing national positions. However, a general debate has been initiated over the priorities of German foreign policy and which institutions will implement it. This debate took place largely 'under wraps' in 1991 because policy-makers were more concerned with the immediate pressures of German unification, the integration of the GDR in the EC, the Gulf and Yugoslav crises and the IGCs. One thing seems clear, however: the Maastricht agreement does not necessarily bind Germany into a common EC foreign policy. In the context of CFSP the motor effect of German unification in driving forward European integration seems to have lost much of its momentum after the Dublin European Council in 1990.

Summary

The FRG remains, as the Baker–Genscher initiative on the introduction of a North Atlantic Cooperation Council (NACC) showed, an important instigator of changes in European relations and in the CSCE institutionalization process. It stands for the widest possible policy of liaison, as shown by its bilateral agreements with the central and east European states. Uncertainty and mistakes in the presentation of German foreign policy have, however, rapidly assumed a fundamental importance, especially when they unsettle other members of the Community. This means that the need for effective coordination in the interests of integration has increased rather than decreased for the FRG government. In contrast to the period before unification there is now a temptation to threaten to 'go it alone'. This was what German 'assertiveness' during the war in the former Yugoslavia was all about. It does not, however, apply to the financing of east European policy. The united Germany is not only politically but also financially stretched, so much so that it is at risk of being over-committed. The federal government is therefore likely to be interested in a continuation of and eventually an increase in intra-EC redistribution of the costs of support for eastern Europe, which will probably influence the German position in the debate on the EC budget.

On the other hand, Germany probably has most interest in an active EC policy towards eastern Europe, including the development of CFSP as an instrument of policy. Here Germany and the UK could work together in spite of different strategies. Both consider it a priority to establish a new political relationship with the Russian Federation and the core members of the CIS that is both durable and treaty-based. London and Bonn are pushing the EC to include the effects of the EFTA enlargement as well as the more difficult eastern enlargements in the discussions concerning EC reforms and budgetary debate.[26]

In the matter of British desires to maintain a long-term US commitment in Europe, the German government has made sure it has included transatlantic cooperation in the Franco-German coordination process. The UK sees the German position as highly ambivalent as regards the institutionalization of the security and the defence policy of the Union. In this sense the British government has criticized the Franco-German proposals for the sharing of duties between NATO and WEU for not being sufficiently well thought through.

The political and financial contribution of Germany to its central and eastern European neighbours will probably increase, but it is unlikely to gain as much influence as was originally feared. The Foreign Affairs Committee of the House of Commons, for example, reached the conclusion that Germany was indeed the most active country in the region but that this did not indicate any kind of new orientation. On the other hand, the German 'EC perspective and accession rhetoric' could prove to be an obstacle to a clear and responsible east European policy on the part of the Community, since the actual political, economical and social problems of the region and also of the EC are much more severe than Bonn has been prepared to admit.

A German *Alleingang* in east European policy would be politically and financially costly and would, as far as the federal German government is concerned, lead in the medium term to a loss in influence rather than a gain. The German *Ostpolitik* has in any case served as a catalyst for joint Franco-German initiatives. For instance, it is envisaged that meetings with the Polish foreign minister will be held annually. In the Weimar declaration of 29 August 1991,[27] the French, German and Polish Foreign Ministers came, rather obliquely, to an understanding on the double strategy of 'deepening in order to widen'. This means that the EC will form 'the core of European institutions' and has to achieve integration before it can realize its aim of opening up the way for new democracies to join. At their second meeting in Bergerac on 24 April 1992 the three foreign ministers stressed the need for a political dialogue 'between the member states of the EC and Poland as well as the other partners of the European treaties'.[28]

The FRG remains the EC state which ties its own destiny most firmly to the political and economic developments in eastern Europe. The speech by former Foreign Minister Genscher 'that in the long run it cannot be to the good of the west if ... the east does badly', has changed from an appeal for assistance to a perceived threat. Germany will continue to put across this point of view both in the EC, where decisions on economic relations will be made, and in the CFSP.

11
CONCLUSIONS

The illusion of a smooth unification

In a formal sense the integration of the former GDR into the European Community through its unification with the existing Federal Republic of Germany ran very smoothly. The legal structures of the FRG and the established EC *acquis* were, with a few exceptions, extended to include east Germany. There were no protracted negotiations over the terms and conditions. In a political sense also the EC enlargement-without-accession ran amazingly smoothly. Germany's Community partners were generally supportive and there were few immediate problems resulting from its increased size. Even the external dimension of unification, in terms of security relations with the USSR and USA and the assimilation of the united Germany into NATO, generally ran much more smoothly than might have been expected, given the importance attributed to the resolution of the German question for more than forty years.

In reality, of course, things are more complicated, as this study has attempted to show. The application of west German and EC legal structures in east Germany could not bring about systemic change from a centralized planned economy to a market economy overnight. It is proving more costly than anticipated and the level of financial transfers to the east is putting the domestic west German consensus under strain; it also has knock-on effects on the rest of the European economy. The FRG's EC partners may have gone along with developments during 1990 and 1991 because of the political imperative of bringing about unification rapidly, but some important issues remain to be resolved. There were those in both Germany and the EC Commission who argued from the outset that the economic transition would not be straightforward. For the most part, however, there was a conspiracy of optimism about the real impact of unification. It was felt more convenient to argue that the outcome of such an unprecedented process was uncertain, rather than make any real attempt to analyse, on a sector-by-sector basis, just what the impact would be. There emerged therefore an illusion that unification and the assimilation of the GDR into the EC could be achieved without disrupting the established order or *acquis*.

Such an illusion was convenient for the federal government in Bonn. The pace of events in the GDR during the winter and spring of 1990 made unification inevitable and there was a belief that the quicker it could be achieved the better. A rapid move towards German monetary union was seen as essential to stem the haemorrhaging of the east German economic lifeblood through migration. From early 1990 there was also a political momentum behind unification. To attempt to swim against this tide or to point to the difficulties and costs of unification was therefore a high-risk political strategy. Bonn was also aware of the window of opportunity offered by the Gorbachev leadership in Moscow to get Soviet endorsement of unification, especially given the unpredictable outcome of the political change underway in the USSR. The attempted putsch in August 1991 proved that this concern was not ill-founded. For Bonn the illusion of a smooth transition helped to lubricate the political wheels of unification which, after forty-one years of division, many might have doubted would ever move again. An accentuation of the problems could have meant a loss of momentum. The illusion was also convenient in that it enabled Bonn to retain control over the process of unification. For Germany's partners it meant that difficult decisions could at least be left until less tumultuous times.

This study has shown that there are real costs involved in unification. Within west Germany the promise of no tax increases to pay for unification proved unsustainable. Once the Chancellor reneged on this pledge, the costs of unification began to threaten the west German consensus on redistribution of wealth, on which the success of the FRG's social market economy has been based. Within east Germany any euphoria quickly gave way to a more realistic view of the prospects for the rapid establishment of a sound, competitive east German industry. The political impact of east German dependence on 'hand-outs' from the west remains uncertain. By 1992 the costs of unification were also beginning to feed through to Germany's partners. Germany's need to stabilize money supply and the fiscal deficit by means of higher interest rates had, by mid-1992, become hard to reconcile with the wish of its

European neighbours, as well as the USA, to take action to revive the European and international economy, culminating in Britain's departure from the ERM and the souring of Anglo-German relations.

In 1990 German unification was a motivating force behind the intensification of the efforts to create a European economic and monetary union, and the most important motivating force behind the initiative to launch a second intergovernmental negotiation on political union. Over two years later the balance looks different. Those who argued for caution on monetary union, including the Bundesbank and large sections of German business, have used the experience with German monetary union and the *Angst* of price instability to reinforce their case. Unification necessarily influences Germany's role in the European economy. The massive financial transfers to the east also affect Germany's willingness to continue to increase its contributions to the EC budget, which impinges upon the debate about the Delors-II package and the future funding of the Community. Unification has also influenced the structure of certain key sectors in the economy and the German approach to regulatory policy. In some sectors this could affect competition within the single market and even EC liberalization efforts. Finally, unification seems certain to have implications for the way in which the Germans and their neighbours see the future role of Germany in general and in the Community in particular.

The impact of the EC on unification

The EC provided a political and economic framework without which it is difficult to see how German unification could have come about. Bonn has always argued that it could only occur within a integrated Europe. There seems little doubt that the USSR (and Germany's other neighbours) would not have been as willing to allow unification to proceed had it not taken place within the context of the EC. But beyond providing this essential political framework the Community's impact on the key decisions on unification was marginal, whether in the political and security aspects, with regard to the *Staatsvertrag* and *Einigungsvertrag*, or even in the field of regulatory policy and competition, in which its competence is most well-developed. Moreover, the fact that the EC, in line with Bonn's wish, provided only token funding in support of structural adjustment in the east meant that it gained no leverage through the power of the purse.

In the medium to long term there may be a greater role for the EC. The convergence criteria laid down, at German insistence, in the Maastricht agreement will force Germany to maintain tight fiscal and monetary policies. But the Bundesbank would in any case have tightened the money supply and raised interest rates in order to regain control over inflation. In the longer term the EC may well intervene to enforce environmental provisions and adopt a tougher line on subsidies.

The impact of unification on the EC

German unification and the IGCs
The impact of unification on the EC was more profound, although it is again important to distinguish between the short- to medium-term effects and the longer-term effects. In the short term unification was a major contributory factor to the acceleration of the process of EMU and created much of the momentum behind the second IGC on political union. The general state of flux in European politics after the dramatic events of 1989 led to a strong desire to ensure unification took place within the context of further European integration. But other more pragmatic and technical issues, such as how to ensure economic convergence before establishing a single currency, rapidly moved back to centre stage. Concerns about the loss of national sovereignty over issues such as foreign policy also came to the fore, and the debate was further complicated by other questions, such as enlargement of the EC.

German unification therefore helped push national governments to make commitments on a political union before they or their publics were clear about what the objectives and content of the union should be, and certainly before public opinion supported it. In early 1990 much less work had been done on EPU than EMU; indeed the whole debate was about creating a Common Foreign and Security Policy for the EC and strengthening its institutions. German unification made the national governments willing to discuss these issues but it did not help resolve any of the differences of view within the EC. As governments wrestled to reach an agreement before the deadline of 31 December 1991, it was necessary to paper over the unresolved differences, with the result that the final product was a bad text. It would be wrong to argue that German unification was in itself responsible for European governments getting ahead of public opinion and concluding an agreement in Maastricht which has subsequently proved difficult to ratify. In the wake of the Danish referendum rejection of the Maastricht agreement it became conventional wisdom that governments had overstepped what European public opinion was ready to accept in terms of a European Union, and the French referendum result confirmed that view. Nevertheless German unification, along with the other momentous political changes that occurred in Europe in 1989 and 1990, certainly pushed the pace of integration. The communiqués of the Strasbourg and Dublin European Councils testify to this in their repeated references to the need for the EC to respond to the changes by consolidation.

The macroeconomic implications
The short-term economic effects of unification were also positive for the Community and the other member states. But the mini-boom of 1990–91 was financed by massive financial transfers from the west to the east of Germany, which introduced inflationary pressures into the German economy, and subsequently into the whole European economy. By 1992 the perception in London was that, at a time when recession was hurting deeply, the hands of the British government were tied because of Britain's membership of the ERM and because German interest rates were high as a direct result of unification. Indirectly, therefore, Britain was seen to be paying a belated price for unification, and the medium-term effects have been negative, particularly after Britain was forced out of the ERM. Even without unification, however, there would have been a need for deflationary policies throughout the EC to meet the convergence criteria for EMU.

In the longer term the impact of unification also seems likely to consolidate the tendency of Germany to favour caution and monetary stability. Germany is likely to remain the anchor of the European economy. But there will be costs in terms of the scope left for other countries to pursue reflationary policies.

Reallocation and the social consensus
The direct costs of unification have also fed through into Germany's tougher position in the debate about the future financing of the Community. In so far as structural funds contribute to economic convergence, or at least to an acceptance of the costs of convergence by the poorer member states, this has a further impact on the prospects for EMU. Germany's stance has put greater pressure on Britain to yield on the question of its rebate on its contributions to the Community budget or, alternatively, Britain and Germany joining forces to cap EC spending.

The costs of unification have also placed tremendous pressure on the established west German consensus, as was seen in the public-sector

127

strikes of spring 1992. How Germany comes to terms with these pressures will affect the nature of the German socioeconomic system and thus indirectly the rest of the EC.

Microeconomic effects

On a microeconomic level unification has had little impact in the short run on the EC. Chapter 5 showed how the German and EC models of regulatory policy were simply extended to include the eastern part of Germany. At both German and EC levels, however, there was no attempt to assess, on a sector-by-sector basis, what the impact of this would be on the east German economy. There was a belief or hope that the invisible hand of the market would bring about the requisite systemic change from central planning to a market economy. With the benefit of hindsight it easy to see why this stood little chance of happening.

This experience allows a number of conclusions. First, the German model of *Ordnungspolitik* has proved to be more flexible than many might have anticipated initially. The overriding concern was to ensure that investment took place in the east German economy. In the process competition was relegated to secondary importance, thus reversing the normal German view of industrial policy. The pressure for a generally more interventionist approach to industrial policy has also mounted as the scale of the structural problems facing east German industry has become apparent.

Second, there has been a *de facto* extension of market dominance to east Germany by west German companies in certain key sectors. The case-studies on energy and financial services clearly demonstrate this. In a few instances the extension of market dominance will make future liberalization of EC-wide markets harder. Having invested on a massive scale in the east German power sector, west German firms will expect to get a return on investment over a period of 10–20 years. This means that major stumbling-blocks have been placed in the path of the introduction of an EC-wide common carriage regime for the power and gas sectors. In most sectors of the economy, however, the opening of the border to west Germany and the EC guarantees competition – indeed it has been too fierce in most east German manufacturing companies.

Third, the Community, in the shape of the Commission, has so far taken a flexible approach to subsidies for east Germany but the pressure for tighter controls seems likely to increase. The internal German debate on the degree of intervention needed to restructure the east German economy was still unresolved at the time of writing. Greater intervention could influence the debate on EC industrial policy. But whatever happens

Bonn will no longer be able to preach to its EC partners about non-intervention: the current policies of the Treuhand are inevitably interventionist. The case of shipbuilding illustrates how the provision of subsidies in east Germany can create tensions, and how the support for east German companies in sensitive sectors can have knock-on effects on the rest of the EC.

The impact on British and German perceptions of the EC

In the immediate aftermath of the fall of the Berlin Wall there was a clear difference between the general approaches of the British and German governments. The German response was to seek to ensure that, following long-established German policy, unification took place within the framework of European integration. There was also a desire to reassure Germany's neighbours and Moscow, by tying Germany into the EC, and to ensure that the unified Germany would not be forced to act alone in response to challenges from the east. Given the uncertainties about developments in central and eastern Europe and the USSR, the best way of doing this was to anchor German foreign policy firmly within the multilateral frameworks of both NATO and the EC's CFSP. The British government under Mrs Thatcher was very keen for the unified Germany to be a member of NATO and held up the 2+4 talks in order to help ensure that this happened, but did not share the Germans' view that their country needed to be anchored in a CFSP as well. Such a policy would have meant submerging Britain's political sovereignty in a European Union, and that was too high a price to pay.

From 1991 onwards, there were signs of convergence in British and German policies on various aspects of EC policy, in part, at least, as a result of unification. This was, for example, the case with regard to the pace of moves towards EMU. Although there is no easy parallel between EMU and GEMU, the lessons of German monetary union had the effect of shifting the political debate within Germany. Germany (again) assumed a policy of caution on EMU with which the British government, by then under John Major, was broadly comfortable. Germany's desire to respond to the interests of its new immediate eastern neighbours seeking membership of the EC also coincided with the British desire to push ahead with bringing both EFTA and the central and east European countries into the EC. The costs of unification also made Germany an ally of the UK in calling for austerity to be extended to the EC budget as well as national budgets.

Conclusions

In the long term, however, these 'tactical' convergences could not disguise the fact that the British and German governments continue to hold very different views on the *finalités* of the Community. Germany still supports European Union and a single European currency, albeit on certain specific conditions, whereas Britain's position is much more conditional. This has been borne out by events following Black Wednesday, with Britain drifting, its commitment to the EC apparently weakened, and Germany anxious to press ahead.

The impact on perceptions of Germany

There is an ambiguity in the EC member states' perceptions of the unified Germany. On the one hand, there is a fear of German dominance, particularly economic dominance, of the Community. Moreover, through its close links with central and eastern Europe Germany will eventually extend its influence throughout that region. On the other hand, there is concern that difficulties in coping with the costs of unification could destabilize the German economy and perhaps even the political system. Any such destabilization would inevitably feed through into other countries.

Such an ambiguity in perceptions of Germany is not new. The question is whether unification has brought about any fundamental shift. It is important to recall that views of Germany are often dependent on the school of thought of the observer (see matrix, Table 11.1). Thus those who tend to be favourably disposed towards European integration will see greater integration as a means of dealing with issues arising from German unification, whether the risk is of German dominance or German weakness. Equally, those who tend to favour the 'realist' school of thought will be sceptical about the ability of integration and European institutions to cope with national ambitions or nationalist solutions to problems, and will seek more traditional solutions such as guaranteeing a balance of power.

This has been reflected in the debate on ratification of Maastricht, in which the earlier predominance of integrationist approaches has given way to more realist views. The case for European Union as a means of anchoring the unified Germany firmly in Europe initially played an important part in the rationale for the two IGCs. By 1992, however, the public debate was focused on issues of immediate concern to each country concerned rather than on such strategic considerations. Yet the desire to anchor Germany into the EC may still weigh on the minds of

Table 11.1 Perceptions of Germany's anticipated strength or weakness after unification

School of thought/ Policy implications	Stronger	Weaker
'Integrationist'	'Central anchor' economic locomotive function	More 'normal' state with equal economic power in Europe
Policy implications	Demand for leadership in EC; integration in a strong EC	Develop strong instruments to overcome problems and reduce possible negative spillover effects for Europe
'Realist'	World power – *économie dominante* in Europe	Unreliable partner
Policy implications	Formation of a counter-coalition	Distancing and search for other fora and allies

many even if they do not say so openly. In some cases, such as in Denmark, realist views have found a clear expression in the sense that concern about German dominance of the Community was used to argue against ratification of the treaty. In Britain unification simply does not figure in the ratification debate. This reflects a parochial concern with national sovereignty but also the fact that the British have never seen European integration as an appropriate response to Germany. Even in Germany concerns about the loss of the Deutschmark or of sovereignty in the Länder are now foremost in people's minds, rather than the idea of integration as a means of responding to unification.

The medium-term effects of unification seem, on balance, to have made Germany more of an equal, weaker, partner than a dominant member of the Community. The problems of dealing with systemic change in the east Germany economy, large regional disparities in economic activity and containing the growing budget deficit have made Germany seem more like a 'normal' member state of the EC. The collapse of east–west trade as a result of the chaotic conditions in the central and east European economies and the CIS has also meant that Germany has not (yet) established an exclusive area of influence in those regions. Possibly as a result there has been relatively little expression of concern about German dominance.

Nevertheless, there have been some areas in which Germany has become more important or a more formidable force, partly in foreign policy (over recognition of Croatia and Slovenia), but primarily in economic terms. Despite the difficulties of absorbing the east German economy, Germany has remained the anchor for the European monetary system. Indeed in order to retain monetary stability the Bundesbank has tightened its policies. This has had a significant effect on the scope left for monetary policies in the other member states. During 1992 the Bundesbank continued to determine European monetary policy, by concentrating on internal 'necessities'. This has, of course, been a fact of life for some time, but in Britain wider sections of public opinion have now come to recognize that membership of the ERM means that decisions taken in Germany have a decisive influence on jobs and growth in Britain.

Long-term prospects
On balance, unification seems to have resulted in the medium term in a weaker rather than a stronger Germany. As regards the longer term, much will depend on whether and how completely the east German economy can be turned around. If it can (and during 1992 the strong growth in construction and service sectors gave at least some grounds for optimism), then the German economy, and possibly also its links with markets in central and eastern Europe, will eventually be strengthened.

Germany's neighbours appear to have responded to its relative weakness by a reduction in the perceived need to contain it through integration in the EC. In the long run, therefore, German unification has probably not significantly changed the balance of views on European integration. There has been a return to the *status quo ante* on European union and those who lost ground during the dramatic political developments of 1989 and 1990 have been able to reassert their more pragmatic, cautious agenda. This includes those in Germany who argued for economic convergence before the establishment of a single European currency. It also holds for those in Britain who were desperately unhappy about the speed and momentum that the European integration movement picked up in 1990.

The outcome of the Maastricht ratification process was unknown at the time of writing. If the agreement is not ratified many questions that had appeared closed will be reopened, including the issue of containment through integration. Those who argued that 1989–90 offered a historic window of opportunity to make the qualitative leap to establish a common foreign and security policy or political union may yet prove to have been correct. But this possibility has not been strong enough to convince the Eurosceptics and adherents of the realist school. Indeed, the issue of German unification has been used by both sides to confirm their existing attitudes.

NOTES

The following abbreviations have been used:
FAZ   Frankfurter Allgemeine Zeitung
FT   Financial Times
SZ   Süddeutsche Zeitung

Chapter 2: The history of the unification process

1 For a more extensive treatment of these points see E. Grabitz and A. von Bogdandy, 'Deutsche Einheit und europäische Integration', in *Neue Juristische Wochenschrift*, 17, 1990, pp. 1073–9; and on Berlin, see Burghardt, 'Berlin in der Europäischen Gemeinschaft' in Gerd Langguth (ed.), *Berlin: Vom Brennpunkt der Teilung zur Brücke der Einheit* (Bonn: Bundeszentrale für politische Bindung, 1990), pp. 256–72.

2 See Presse- und Informationsamt der Bundesregierung, *Bulletin* (hereafter *Bulletin*), no. 56, 22 March 1957, pp. 473–9.

3 See speech by Delors to the European Parliament, 17 January 1990, reproduced in *Europa-Archiv*, 11, 1990, p. D273.

4 This interpretation was confirmed in a Constitutional Court ruling of 31 July 1973.

5 See Jürgen Habermas in *Die nachholende Revolution* (Frankfurt am Main: Suhrkamp Verlag, 1990), p. 180.

6 See 'Von Wiedervereinigung keine Rede', *FAZ*, 11 November 1989.

7 Such was the argument used by British Foreign Minister Douglas Hurd following a visit to Berlin, see SZ, 17 November 1989.

8 Genscher assured his Polish counterpart, Skubiszewski, during his visit to Poland, that there would be no Bonn initiative on reunification, see *SZ*, 11/12 November 1989.

9 *FT*, 5 December 1989.

10 Karl Kaiser, *Deutschlands Vereinigung: Die internationalen Aspekte* (Bergisch Gladbach: Gustav Lübbe Verlag, 1991), pp. 45ff.

11 This was the title of his speech in Davos; see *Bulletin*, no. 21, 6 February 1990, pp. 165ff.

12 From Mann's speech to students in Hamburg in 1953.

13 *FAZ*, 20 November 1989 (press conference in Paris).

14 Horst Teltschik, *329 Tage* (Berlin: Siedler Verlag, 1991).

15 EC Commission, *Bulletin of the European Communities*, no. 12, 1989, p. 14. This statement followed very closely the formula adopted in the letter on German unity sent by the FRG to the USSR on the signing of the Moscow Treaty of August 1970.

16 Ibid., no. 10, 1989, pp. 114–23.

17 See her speech at the Guildhall, London, reported in *SZ*, 15 November 1989.

18 See *Agence Europe*, no. 5177, 22/23 January 1990. This would have meant preferential treatment for the GDR over other official applicants for the EC.

19 Dominic Lawson, 'Saying the Unsayable about the Germans', in *Spectator*, 14 July 1990.

20 See *The Independent on Sunday*, 15 July 1990. The six experts were Lord Dacre (Hugh Trevor-Roper), Professor Norman Stone (Oxford University), Timothy Garton Ash, George Urban, Professor Fritz Stern (Columbia University) and Professor Gordon Craig (Harvard University). See also Gordon Craig, 'Die Chequers-Affaire von 1990', in *Vierteljahreshefte für Zeitgeschichte*, 4 (1991), pp. 611–23.

21 Willy Brandt, *Begegnungen und Einsichten* (Munich, Zurich: Hoffmann and Campe, 1978), p. 341.

22 Teltschik, op. cit., p. 179.

23 See *Europa-Archiv*, 11, 1990, p. D283.

24 Quoted by Teltschik, op. cit., p. 109.

25 Interview with *Wall Street Journal*, 26 January 1990.

26 *Europa-Archiv*, 5, 1990, pp. D127–36.

27 Teltschik, op. cit., p. 147.

28 Speech in Mainz, published in *Bulletin*, no. 54, 2 June 1989, pp. 481–8.

29 See Teltschik, op. cit., p. 14.

30 *SZ*, 1 February 1990.

31 *FAZ*, 14 February 1990.

32 Teltschik, op. cit., p. 144.

33 *Die Welt*, 20 February 1990; also reported in *The Times*, 20 February 1990.

34 *Bulletin*, no. 40, 27 March 1990, p. 312.

35 Ibid., no. 54, 8 May 1990, p. 423.

36 Ibid., no. 93, 18 July 1990.

37 *Europa-Archiv*, 24, 1990, pp. 653f.

38 *Bulletin*, no. 134, 16 November 1990, pp. 1394f.

39 *Europa-Archiv*, 24, 1990, pp. D656–64.
40 For a detailed account of the process seen from the point of view of an insider, and on the role of the EC in German unification generally, see David Spence, *Enlargement without Accession: The EC's Response to German Unification*, RIIA Discussion Paper No. 36, London, 1991.
41 Doc. A3–183/90, 9 July 1990.
42 COM 90(400), I–IV.
43 Nine legislative measures were proposed on the internal market; two each on external trade, agriculture, fisheries, the environment and nuclear safety and transport; and one each on energy, structural, and training and social policies. No proposals were found to be necessary for research and development, telecommunications or coal and steel.
44 The ad hoc group sat for a total of 126 hours in 22 sessions between 3 September and 22 November. The external aspects, almost exclusively external trade, took up most time; much of the detail concerning agriculture was dealt with in separate, parallel negotiations. In spite of very unreliable statistics, environmental issues were less problematic than external trade, agricultural quotas (especially sugar) or subsidies. See case-studies in Chapters 6–9.
45 See EP-Informationsbüro Deutschland (ed.), *Europäisches Parlament und deutsche Einheit* (Bonn, 1990), Annex S2.

Chapter 3: Representation in the European Parliament

1 See the conclusions of the Council at the special summit of heads of state and governments, held in Dublin on 28 April 1990, COM90(400), Commission of the EC, vol. 1, p. 1.
2 See European Parliament, PE 141.105 and amendments, Brussels, 18/19 June 1990.
3 The Donnelly Committee: see EP, *Interim Report of the Temporary Committee on the implications of German unification for the European Community*, Rapporteur, Alan Donnelly, Doc. A3–183/90, 9 July 1990.
4 EP, *Resolution on the implications of German unification for the European Community*, 12 July 1990; see *Official Journal of the European Communities*, C231, 17 September 1990, pp. 154–63.
5 EP, *Report of the Committee on the Rules of Procedure on the insertion of a new rule on transitional provisions concerning observers from the territory of the former GDR*, Rapporteur, Mark Galle, Doc. A3–0250/90/ rev., 19 October 1990.
6 EP, *Standing Orders* (6th edition), 1991, Art. 136a, p. 103.
7 On the number of observers, the Donnelly Committee's resolution recommended 18, on condition that this figure should not predetermine the final decision.

8 In almost every parliamentary grouping there were those who did not wish Germany to have greater representation than before, in order to avoid the sensitive issue of the distribution of seats. Others (e.g. Blaney, Rainbow, Ireland) considered the observer status to be unacceptable and undemocratic because it meant that for four years the east German people would not be 'properly' represented. Some MEPs (like Veil, LDR, France), stressed that the outcome was not satisfactory on legal and democratic grounds, and that an intervention by the European Court of Justice could not be ruled out, even if this did not seem likely on political grounds. There were also some (such as Cot, Socialists, France) who insisted upon interpreting the status very strictly. The then President of the Parliament, Baron Crespo, believed that the presence of observers had been accepted purely because there was no other solution at that time, but that the best solution would have been for the German MEPS to have resigned and for new European elections to have been held in the Federal Republic.

9 Each country would have a minimum of six delegates, to be increased according to population. Thus France would have 86 votes, Italy and the UK 87 and the FRG 102.

10 A German MEP represents around 760,000 voters; with an increase to 99 MEPs each would represent 790,000 voters; an Irish MEP, on the other hand, represents only 240,000 voters, and in the special case of Luxembourg there is one MEP for about 60,000 voters.

11 The voting was 240 for and 47 against, with 47 abstentions. On the proposed increase of German seats by 18, 241 voted for and 62 against, with 39 abstentions. See EP, *Resolution on democratic representation in the European Parliament of the 16 million new German citizens*, Proceedings of the EC. no. 3–409; see also *Official Journal of the European Communities*, C280, 28 October 1991, p. 94.

12 *Treaty on European Union*, Declaration on the number of members of the Commission and the European Parliament.

Chapter 4: Macroeconomic implications

1 Others have also argued that the ERM is half-baked, drawing the conclusion, however, that EMU should therefore be brought about quickly.

2 Reproduced in *Europa-Archiv*, 10, 1989, pp. D283–304, here D288f.

3 Treaty of Economic, Currency and Social Union between the Federal Republic of Germany and the German Democratic Republic, reproduced in *Bulletin*, no. 63, pp. 517–44, Bonn, 18 May 1990.

4 Immediately after unification, figures on migration from east Germany were no longer recorded but it is quite apparent that the desired impact of unification in terms of stemming the tide was not realized. The Deutsches Institut für Wirtschaftsforschung (DIW) calculated that in the first year

after GEMSU some 360,000 east Germans moved westwards, see *DIW-Wochenbericht*, 32/91, 8 August 1991, p. 449.

5 Reproduced in Europa-Archiv, 11, 1990, 10 June 1990, p. D283.

6 SEC(90)1138, 14 June 1990, paras. 8–12.

7 This pattern of consumer preferences turned around at the start of 1992: east German consumers began to buy far more products made in the new Bundesländer. Some of the worst fears that east Germany would become a distribution network for west German and other western products do not seem to have been realized, at least in the food manufacturing sector (see Chapter 8).

8 See *Herbstgutachten der Arbeitsgemeinschaft deutscher Wirtschaftswissenschaftlicher Forschungsinstitute e.V.*, reproduced in *DIW-Wochenbericht*, 42–43/91, 24 October 1991, p. 595.

9 See Bundesanstalt für Arbeit, *Eckwerte des Arbeitsmarktes für Juni 1992 im Bundesgebiet Ost*.

10 Survey conducted by the Deutsches Institut für Wirtschaftsforschung and the Institut für Weltwirtschaft. See *DIW-Wochenbericht*, 39–40/91, 29 September 1991, especially pp. 559–65.

11 Ibid., 32/91, 8 August 1991, p. 449.

12 Ibid., 18–19/91, 3 May 1991, pp. 237 and 244. By comparison with 1991 a substantial rise in investment was expected for 1992.

13 See Daniel Gros and Alfred Steinherr, 'Macroeconomic management in the new Germany: implications for the EMS and EMU', in W. Heisenberg (ed.), *German Unification in European Perspective* (Brussels: Brassey's, 1991), pp. 166ff.

14 See *DIW-Wochenbericht*, 7/92, pp. 80f.

15 See *The Community and German Unification*, COM(90)400, vol I, pp. 14–17, Brussels, 21 August 1990.

16 See, for example, *OECD Economic Outlook*, pp. 105–9; Jochen Michaelis and Alexander Spermann, 'Investitionen, Sozialpakt für den Aufschwung, Gewinnbeteiligung – Lösungen für Ostdeutschland?', in *Wirtschaftsdienst*, 12/1991, pp. 614–22.

17 See *OECD Economic Outlook*, pp. 50ff.

18 However, the transitional provisions and derogations to EC rules only applied until 1992 in most cases, in some until 1995, and, compared with previous accessions, were relatively minor. In addition, GDR products to which derogations applied could only be distributed within the new Länder and not in other areas of the EC.

19 See *Agence Europe*, no. 5455, 20 March 1991.

20 See 'Extracts of the debate in the Bundestag on the Maastricht resolutions' in *Das Parlament*, no. 52–3, 20/27 December 1991, pp. 1–9. Rather different views which were later reported, primarily those of the Länder administrations, remained the exception, despite the growing public debate.

21 Art. 104b; Protocol on the excessive deficit procedure.

22 See *Monatsberichte der Deutschen Bundesbank*, February 1992, pp. 45–6; *FT*, 29 January 1992; *Die Zeit*, 7 February 1992; *FAZ*, 8 February 1992; *Handelsblatt*, 24 February 1992.

23 See Lothar Müller, 'Sackgasse zur Europäischen Wirtschafts- und Währungsunion,' in *Europa-Archiv*, 8/1991, pp. 247–54; and also Wolfgang Neumann, *Auf dem Weg zu einer Europäischen Wirtschafts- und Währungsunion* (Stuttgart: Deutscher Sparkassenverlag, 1991), pp. 50–54 and pp. 117–37 (British Treaty text).

24 See *FT*, 12 December 1991.

25 See, for example, Gustav A. Horn, Wolfgang Scheremet and Rudolf Ziner, *Domestic and International Macroeconomic Effects of German Economic and Monetary Union*, DIW Discussion Paper No. 26, p. 51.

26 See the Experts' Report in *OECD Economic Survey 1990/91 for Germany*, pp. 602f., Paris, autumn 1991; also 'If Germany sneezes, the rest of Europe catches a cold', *Guardian*, 17 January 1992.

27 See *The Community and German Unification*, op. cit., vol. 1, p. 15.

28 See *Die Zeit*, 27 December 1991. Foreign investors have an interest in public borrowing, with long maturities, in contrast to German investors.

29 See *DIW-Wochenbericht*, vol. 18–19, 1991, p. 244.

30 See *Herbstgutachten* 1991, op. cit., p. 613.

31 See *Monatsberichte der Deutschen Bundesbank*, December 1991, p. 43.

32 The targeted growth of the M3 money supply (currency plus sight deposits, time deposits of less than four years and savings deposits with a statutory period of notice) was 4–6% for 1990, 3–5% for 1991 and 3.5–5.5% for 1992.

33 See *FAZ*, 11 February 1991.

34 See, for example, *FT*, 20 and 21/22 December 1991.

35 See *FAZ*, 24 December 1991 and *FT*, 11 February 1992.

36 See *FT*, 17 July 1992.

37 By contrast, the French franc succeeded in resisting market speculation, because France's policy of stable money tied to the Deutschmark was credible and its economy was fundamentally stronger than Britain's. There was also a greater recognition of the links between Maastricht and German unification. Other weak currencies suffered like sterling from the pressure within currency markets – the peseta was realigned, and the lira was also forced out of the ERM – but in neither Italy nor Spain was support for ratification weakened as a result.

Chapter 5: Impact on German and EC regulatory frameworks

1 *FAZ*, 2 March 1990.

2 Some 40% of its production was still using the Siemens–Martin process

which had been phased out in Japan in the 1960s and in western Europe during the 1970s. Only 40% of plants used productive continuous casting techniques, as opposed to traditional, less efficient ingot casting and rolling methods.

3 See statement by Gieske of RWE in *FAZ*, 25 April 1990.

4 See *International Herald Tribune*, 30 March 1990.

5 See *FAZ*, 18 April 1990.

6 See *The Times*, 25 May 1990.

7 See *FAZ*, 4 July 1990.

8 See, for example, report of the *Monopolkommission*, reported in *FAZ*, 5 July 1990.

9 See *FAZ*, 28 October 1991.

10 The idea for such undertakings came from the experience of dealing with the effects of the industrial restructuring process in the Ruhr steel-making areas during the recession in the sector in the 1980s, and followed a scheme used in Hattingen in the Ruhr.

11 See, for example, Kolbe, 'Sanierungsfall Treuhand: Plädoyer für eine vorübergehende Industriepolitik im Osten' (unpublished paper).

12 See Deutsches Institut für Wirtschaftsforschung, *Wochenbericht*, 41, 1991, 10 October 1991, pp. 575–9; also '*Frühjahrsgutachten 1992 des Arbeitskreises wirtschaftswissenschaftlicher Forschungsinstitute e.V.*, in *DIW-Wochenbericht*, 16–17, 1992, 16 August 1992.

13 The taxes consisted of a solidarity payment of 7.5% on income tax and corporation tax for one year. This was calculated to raise an estimated DM11bn in additional revenue each year. The tax on oil was raised by 3% (DM2.2bn in revenue), the tax on cigarettes increased (DM1.3bn in revenue), and VAT was increased by 1%, raising the standard rate in the FRG in line with the agreed EC targets.

14 As Chapter 2 has shown, this was indeed what the federal government had wanted, in order to smooth negotiations on the GDR's accession into the Community; it would otherwise have faced strong resistance from its EC partners, especially the southern member states.

15 Speech in Strasbourg, 12 February 1992, reported in *EC News*, no. 2, 17 February 1992, p. 4.

Chapter 6: Case-study – financial services

1 The Staatsbank, the Bank für Land und Nährungsgüterwirtschaft, the Deutsche Außenhandelsbank, the Genossenschaftskassen für Handwerk und Gewerbe, the Sparkassen, and the Postsparkassen. For a comprehensive description of the banking structure in the GDR, see Ulrike Dennig, 'Die Finanzstruktur in den neuen Bundesländern', in *Wirtschaftsdienst*, 1991/III.

2 This is Ulrike Dennig's argument, op. cit.

3 From the perspective of both the Commission and the member states, the implementation of the Merger Control Regulation (EEC No. 4064/89) of 21 December 1989 (which came into force in September 1990), and the enforcement of EC competition law, are crucial to the discussion of future mergers. The refusal of both the British and the German governments to allow the Commission exclusive competence under this regulation to sanction mergers should be taken into account in assessing both potential British and German interests in the development of the financial services sector within the five eastern Länder. Article 21(3) of the regulation leaves with member governments powers to apply their national criteria in some respects, including the operation of prudential regulations in sectors such as financial services.

4 See, for example, Klaus Krummich, 'Strukturwandel in der ostdeutschen Kreditwirtschaft', in *Sparkasse*, 10/91, vol. 108.

5 See Commission of the European Communities, *Twentieth Report on Competition Policy* (Brussels, Luxembourg, 1991), pp. 41–3, for a report on how this and other major individual cases were handled.

6 See Peter Lee, 'Common goals, divided loyalties', in *Euromoney*, February 1992.

7 For example, in 1991, EGIT, a fund placed by County NatWest Wood MacKenzie, bought 47% of Dresdner Beton. The firm is now 51% owned by management, 2% by the Treuhandanstalt.

8 See *Twentieth Report on Competition Policy*, op. cit.

9 See *SZ*, 21–22 July 1990.

10 Ibid., 22/23 June 1991, 'Staatsanwalt ermittelt wegen Allianz-Deal'.

11 See *FT*, 30 August 1991.

12 See 'Barclays goes big in Germany', *Banking World*, November 1990.

13 See 'The single European market: survey of the UK financial services industry', *Bank of England Quarterly Bulletin*, vol. 29, no. 3, August 1989.

Chapter 7: Case-study – the energy sector

1 See *Agence Europe*, no. 1756, 29 January 1992.

2 See COM238(88), *The Internal Energy Market*.

3 For an in-depth discussion on energy and the Single European Market, see *A Single European Market in Energy*, RIIA/Science Policy Research Unit, 1989. Energy objectives for the Community adopted by the Council mention the need for 'greater integration, free from barriers to trade, of the internal energy market with a view to improving security of supply, reducing costs and improving economic competitiveness', *Official Journal*, No. C241, 25 August 1986.

4 See COM(90)365 final, 13 November 1990, *Specific Actions for Vigorous Energy Efficiency*, Commission Communication to the Council.

5   See *Marktöffnung und Wettbewerb*, 2nd Report, 'Die Stromwirtschaft', Deregulierungskommission, Bonn, March 1991.

6   See European Parliament Working Document, *Energy in the GDR: the situation now and in the future*, EP, DG Research, Notice to Members of the Temporary Committee to consider the impact of the process of German reunification on the European Community, Luxembourg, 8 May 1990, PE 141.761.

7   As at end of 1988 – in an official statement by the Federal Economics Ministry of 1 April 1992, the level of high btu gas reserves as of 1 January 1991 stood at 46.8 BCM.

8   The EC's goal was for a 50% Europe-wide reduction in the use of lignite by 1998. Given the anticipated fall in domestic consumption, emissions of sulphur dioxide were expected to fall by over 30% by the same date.

9   As opposed to federal government support for increased use – on environmental grounds – in recognition of the limited availability of both fossil and mineral resources and their pollutants, a lack of what the government considered to be 'suitable' alternatives, and not least price competitiveness – see *Energiebericht*, 24 September 1986.

10 See *Energy in the GDR*, op. cit.

11 For a full account of developments in the electricity sector in the former GDR in the transitional period of 1989/90, see Mez, Jänicke and Pöschk, *Die Energiesituation in der vormaligen DDR* (Bonn: Sigma, 1991).

12 See *Tätigkeitsbericht des Bundeskartellamtes*, 1989/90 (July 1990).

13 The *Elektrizitätsversorgungsunternehmen* – electricity supply companies.

14 See Peter Brackley, *Energy and Environmental Terms: A Glossary*, Joint Energy Programme/Policy Studies Institute/RIIA Energy Papers No. 24 (Aldershot: Gower, 1988).

15 For an outline of EC proposals and an explanation of open access see *A Single European Market in Energy*, op. cit., pp. 27–9.

16 According to a report in the *SZ* (6 May 1991), PreußenElektra AG, Hanover, made an attractive offer to the Stendal *Stadtwerke* for a 51% majority shareholding, which, if accepted, could act as a skeleton compromise agreement for use in the disputes between other *Stadtwerke* and the Treuhand and large West German energy firms. The offer was made subject to the *Stadtwerke* being able to operate competitively and withdrawing their test suit filed against the Treuhand in March 1991 on behalf of 52 towns in Saxony Anhalt. This concerned the provision for the electricity company to take 49% of the shares, whereas the municipal authorities wanted the benefits of the investments to be transferred to themselves free of charge.

17 However, even though the Federal Cartel Office places the strictest emphasis on competition as a yardstick for assessing *Ordnungspolitik*, decisions can be overruled by the Ministry of Economics on public policy

grounds. For further discussion of EC merger control and its application in member states, see Heinrich Hölzer, 'Merger Control', in Peter Montagnon (ed.), *European Competition Policy* (London: RIIA/Pinter, 1990).

18 In July 1991 British Gas acquired a 25.5% stake in the new gas distribution company to serve Leipzig. This was to be in partnership with VEW who also have 25.5%, with the remaining 49% controlled by the local administrations. In June it had acquired similar shares in Halle, together with the 5% offer in VNG supplying gas to the whole of the GDR. These cities have 'opted out' of regional supply arrangements and have established their own *Stadtwerke* for gas distribution within the city – although the regional companies retain the responsibility for supply to the point of distribution.

19 Section 24(1) of the *Gesetz gegen Wettbewerbsbeschränkungen* (Law Prohibiting Restraints of Competition) of 27 July 1957 relies on the concept of market domination as the central criterion to identify anti-competitive mergers. This law is also known as the *Kartellgesetz (KartG)*.

20 See Kurt E Markert, 'German Anti-Trust Law and the Internationalization of Markets', in *World Competition*, March 1990.

21 Gazprom had over the years become disenchanted with Ruhrgas's monopoly position over Soviet gas.

22 See James Ball in *Gas Matters*, 16 December 1991.

23 See Jonathan P Stern, *Third Party Access in European Gas Industries: Regulation-driven or Market-led?* (London: RIIA, 1992).

24 See *FAZ*, 22 May 1992.

25 See *Energiewirtschaft*, no. 5129.

Chapter 8: Case-study – agriculture

1 See EP Temporary Committee's Working Document on 'The consequences of German unification for the EC's agricultural and fisheries policy'.

2 The GDR was self-sufficient in meat, milk and cheese; it exported cattle and in 1990 produced four million tonnes more grain than it consumed.

3 Since unification there has been a resurgence in the demand by eastern consumers for their old products, which have improved enormously in terms of both quality control and packaging. However, this demand has not so far been met by the large (west) German supermarket chains, which seldom source their products in the east, even for eastern branches.

4 The Commission had suggested 800,000 tonnes, the Federal Republic and the GDR 900,000; 870,000 tonnes was finally agreed as a compromise.

Chapter 9: Case-study – shipbuilding

1 See Commission of the EC, *The European Community and German Unification*, EC Bulletin, Supplement 4/90, Luxembourg, 1990.

2 See Donnelly Committee Report: European Parliament, *Interim Report of the Temporary Committee on the Implications of German Unification for the European Community*, Rapporteur, Alan Donnelly, Doc. A3/133/90, 9 July 1990.

3 See *Debates of the European Parliament*, 9.7.92, No. 3–420/271.

4 See Chapter 10.

5 According to information supplied by DMS on 16 December 1991.

6 Ibid.

7 See *Die Zeit*, 6 March 1992.

8 See *VWD-Europa*, 6 March 1991.

9 The available 1990 shipbuilding capacity for all the yards in the former GDR was estimated to be 545,000 cgt in a detailed study made for the Commission by an independent consultant. The German government's proposed reductions (a total of 327,000 cgt) are as follows: Mathias Thesen Werft, 100,000 cgt; Warnow Werft, 85,000 cgt; Peene Werft, 35,000cgt; Volkswerft, 85,000 cgt; Elbe Werft Bolzenburg, 22,000 cgt. (Cgt = compensated gross tonnes, a measure of the amount of work involved in building a vessel.) These cuts mean that Rosslauer Schiffswerft, as well as Neptun Werft, will be irreversibly closed for the new building of sea-going vessels.

10 See *Debates of the European Parliament*, No. 3–420/271, 9.7.92, 'Aid to Shipbuilding'.

11 See Alan Donnelly, op. cit.

12 See *The European Community and German Unification*, op. cit.

13 See *Guardian*, 3 December 1992.

14 See House of Commons Parliamentary Debate on Aid to Shipbuilding, European Standing Committee B, 18 November 1992.

Chapter 10: External implications

1 See EPC Declaration, 2 October 1990, in *Agence Europe*, no. 5341, 3 October 1990, p. 3.

2 *Bulletin of the EC*, 12/1989, p. 15.

3 For the historical dimension, see Gregor Schöllgen, *Die Macht in der Mitte Europas. Stationen deutscher Außenpolitik von Friedrich dem Großen bis zur Gegenwart* (Munich: C.H. Beck, 1992); and for a current discussion of the problems of a central location see Richard von Weizsäcker, 'Meilenstein Maastricht' in *FAZ*, 13 April 1992.

4 This is illustrated by the German debate over further support for nuclear weapons. See also, on the migration issue, the excellent report of the

Foreign Affairs Committee: 'First Report: Central and Eastern Europe: Problems of the Post-Communist Era', vol. I, London 1991 (House of Commons Version 1991–92), here pp. XXXIVff. and XV–XVII.

5 'Not a bridge, not the centre'; see the historian Michael Stürmer in *FAZ*, 3 March 1992.

6 See COM(90)400, final, Vol. I, p. 49.

7 This applied both to agricultural and manufactured goods which were not subject to cream-skimming, as well as to European Coal and Steel Community products.

8 The countries which had greatest difficulty in supplying were the former Soviet republics and Yugoslavia and its successor states.

9 At the start of 1991 exports to the former CMEA states fell between 47% and 91%, see Table 10.2.

10 In mid-1991, the EC countries accounted for 18.2% of imports into the new Länder and 16.8% of their exports, compared with 62.9% and 65.1% for Central and Eastern Europe.

11 See Eurostat, *External Trade*, monthly statistics 5 (1991), pp. 96–101 and 185–7.

12 See the programme *Gemeinschaftswerk Aufschwung Ost*.

13 Initially there was no ceiling, but a DM5bn ceiling had to be introduced at the start of 1992 (DM100m for any single contract) because the rush of applications had already risen to DM33.5bn by October 1991.

14 See Bundesministerium für Wirtschaft, *Ausgewählte Wirtschaftsdaten zur Lage in den neuen Bundesländern*, 6 March 1992, p. 18.

15 See speech by Helmut Kohl on 9 October 1991, in *Bulletin*, no. 114, pp. 897ff. Figures include the costs of the withdrawal of Soviet armed forces.

16 See Foreign Affairs Committee, op. cit., p. XLI.

17 Werner Link, 'Die außenpolitische Staatsraison der Bundesrepublik Deutschland', in Manfred Funke et al. (eds), *Demokratie und Diktatur* (Bonn, 1987), p. 406.

18 Joint communiqué of Kohl and Mitterrand of 18 April 1990, reproduced in *Europa-Archiv*, 11, 1990, p. D283.

19 See Karl W. Deutsch, *Political Community and the North Atlantic Area* (Princeton, NJ: Princeton University Press, 1957).

20 In October 1990 only 35% of Germans, as compared with 69% of the British people, were for a European Rapid Deployment Force; see EC Commission, *Eurobarometer*, no. 34, December 1990, Brussels, 1990, p. 41.

21 See Christian Deubner, 'Die EG und Jugoslawiens Bürgerkrieg', SWP-IP2726, October 1991; Geoffrey Edwards, 'European Responses to the Yugoslav Crisis: An Interim Assessment', in Reinhardt Rummel (ed.), *Toward Political Union: Planning a Common Foreign Policy in the European Community* (Baden-Baden: Nomos Verlag, 1992), pp. 165–89,

especially p. 176; and Scott Anderson, 'Western Europe and the Gulf War', in ibid., pp. 151–64.

22 (1) The Franco-German initiative of 14 April 1990 (before the Dublin special European Council meeting), which was seen by Bonn and Paris as, among other things, a signal for a permanent commitment by Germany to the EC and for the continuation of the privileged relationship between Paris and Bonn; (2) a joint communiqué to the President of the Council, 6 December 1990, which endorsed the established policy in advance of the Rome European Council meeting; (3) the joint Dumas/Genscher initiative of 4 February 1991 which proposed the areas of common action under the CFSP; (4) the Franco–German–Spanish Foreign Ministers' communiqué of 11 October 1991 on a European defence identity; and (5) the joint Kohl/Mitterrand communiqué of 14 October 1991 on CFSP to the President of the Council, Minister President Lubbers, which endorsed the established line in advance of Maastricht, but was largely noted for its proposal to establish a European 'corps'.

23 See the British–Italian proposal of November 1991, reproduced in *Europe Documents*, no. 1735, 5 October 1991.

24 See, for example, the speech by Chancellor Kohl to the German Bundestag on 4 September 1991 in *Bulletin*, no. 95, p. 759.

25 See Françoise de La Serre, 'Hat die Europäische Gemeinschaft eine Ostpolitik?', in Christian Deubner (ed.), *Die Europäische Gemeinschaft in einem neuen Europa: Herausforderungen und Strategien* (Baden-Baden, 1991), p. 201.

26 See Anna Michalski and Helen Wallace, *The European Community: The Challenge of Enlargement* (London: RIIA, 1992).

27 *Bulletin*, no. 92, 3 September 1991, pp. 734ff.

28 Ibid., no. 45, 30 April 1992, pp. 410f.

Also in this series

The Bundesbank: Germany's Central Bank in the International Monetary System
Ellen Kennedy

This is a key paper for anyone wanting to make sense of the new Europe. The Bundesbank is crucial for the processes of both German and European economic and monetary union. It may provide the model for any future European Central Bank or 'Eurofed'. To understand the implications of this for the future of European monetary integration one must also understand the history and structure of the Bundesbank, its ethos and its objectives. This timely paper examines these issues and in particular how the Bundesbank has reacted to international pressure.

'A first-rate study that squeezes a great deal of material into not very many pages.' – *Foreign Affairs*

Contents
1 Introduction
2 The Bundesbank: ethos, organization, powers
3 The Bundesbank in the German political system
4 The Bundesbank in the international economic system
5 The European Monetary System
6 The Bundesbank in a changing world

The author
Ellen Kennedy is Associate Professor of Political Science in the University of Pennsylvania. She has also taught at the Universities of Manchester, York and London and at the Albert-Ludwigs-Universität in Freiburg, where she was a fellow of the Alexander von Humboldt Foundation. She has written widely on German political culture and political theory.

RIIA/PINTER PUBLISHERS

Britain, Germany and 1992:
The Limits of Deregulation

Stephen Woolcock, Michael Hodges
and Kristin Schreiber

This study is based on research by the Royal Institute of International Affairs and the Institut für Europäische Politik, Bonn, in association with the Anglo-German Foundation for the Study of Industrial Society.

The volume addresses two main questions: what kind of single European market will emerge as a result of the 1992 process, and what effect will its creation have on the traditional approaches of Britain and Germany towards the regulation of markets? The book consists of case-studies of five areas in which 1992 is likely to have a particularly significant impact: mergers and acquisitions, public procurement, technical standards, telecommunications and financial services. The authors conclude that in these areas 1992 will result in a net deregulation of European markets, but that, at the same time, old regulations will need to be replaced in some instances by new, European-level regulations if the objectives of the single market are to be realized.

'Very impressive analysis of the different approaches to 1992 of Britain and Germany.' – *The Higher*

The authors
Stephen Woolcock is a Research Fellow with the European Programme of the Royal Institute of International Affairs. Kristin Schreiber is a Researcher at the Institut für Europäische Politik, Bonn. Michael Hodges is Senior Lecturer in International Relations at the London School of Economics and Political Science and is an Associate Research Fellow at the Royal Institute of International Affairs.

RIIA/PINTER PUBLISHERS